Racing Rivals

The Hamilton vs. Rosberg Story

Etienne Psaila

Racing Rivals: The Hamilton vs. Rosberg Story

Copyright © 2024 by Etienne Psaila. All rights reserved.

First Edition: **November 2024**

No part of this publication may be reproduced, distributed, or transmitted in any form or by any means, including photocopying, recording, or other electronic or mechanical methods, without the prior written permission of the publisher, except in the case of brief quotations embodied in critical reviews and certain other non-commercial uses permitted by copyright law.

ISBN: 978-1-923361-63-8

Table of Contents

Introduction: The Making of a Modern Rivalry

Chapter 1: Early Lives and Racing Origins

Chapter 2: Karting Days—Where Friendship Began

Chapter 3: Climbing the Ranks—Paths Diverge

Chapter 4: Early Formula 1 Careers

Chapter 5: Reuniting at Mercedes—Teammates Again

Chapter 6: The 2013 Season—Setting the Stage

Chapter 7: The 2014 Season—Rivalry Ignites

Chapter 8: The 2015 Season—Tensions Rise

Chapter 9: The 2016 Season—The Final Showdown

Chapter 10: Behind the Scenes—Team Dynamics and Politics

Chapter 11: The Psychological Battle

Chapter 12: Rosberg's Retirement—An Unexpected Farewell

Chapter 13: Aftermath and Individual Paths

Chapter 14: The Legacy of a Rivalry

Chapter 15: Lessons in Competition and Friendship

Conclusion: The Enduring Tale of Hamilton vs. Rosberg

Introduction: The Making of a Modern Rivalry

In the high-octane world of Formula 1 racing, rivalries are as inevitable as the screech of tires on asphalt. Yet, few have captured the imagination of fans and the attention of the world like the rivalry between Lewis Hamilton and Nico Rosberg. This is not just a story of two exceptional drivers vying for supremacy on the track; it's a tale of friendship, ambition, and the complexities that arise when personal and professional lives intertwine.

Overview of the Hamilton-Rosberg Rivalry

Lewis Hamilton and Nico Rosberg first crossed paths as young karting prodigies, their shared dreams forging a bond that would carry them through the ranks of motorsport. They laughed together, celebrated victories side by side, and envisioned futures where both could stand atop the podium. But as they ascended to the pinnacle of Formula 1 and became teammates at Mercedes, the dynamics shifted dramatically. The camaraderie of youth gave way to the fierce competitiveness of adulthood, and their once-strong friendship began to fray under the relentless pressure to win.

Their rivalry unfolded over four intense seasons from 2013 to 2016, a period marked by thrilling races, strategic mind games, and moments of high drama that left fans worldwide on the edge of their seats. The battle between Hamilton and Rosberg was not merely about who could drive faster; it was a psychological duel that tested their limits and reshaped their identities both on and off the track.

Significance in Formula 1 History

The Hamilton-Rosberg rivalry stands as one of the most compelling narratives in modern Formula 1 history. It harkens back to legendary duels like those between Ayrton Senna and Alain Prost or James Hunt and Niki Lauda, yet it possesses a unique modern twist. In an era dominated by technological advancements and team strategies, their personal conflict brought a human element back to the sport, reminding audiences of the raw passion and emotion that fuel racing at its highest level.

Their battles had far-reaching implications for Formula 1. They pushed technological boundaries as Mercedes sought to give each driver the competitive edge, leading to innovations that have influenced the sport's evolution. The rivalry also prompted discussions about team dynamics, driver welfare, and the psychological pressures faced by athletes in high-stakes environments. In essence, their story is not just about two drivers but about the very nature of competition and excellence in the modern age.

The Friendship-Turned-Rivalry Narrative

At the heart of this story lies a profound irony: the very friendship that once united Hamilton and Rosberg became the foundation of their rivalry. Their shared history added layers of complexity to their competition. They knew each other's strengths, weaknesses, and vulnerabilities, which made their battles intensely personal. The journey from friends to rivals—and perhaps back again—is a poignant exploration of how ambition can both connect and divide.

Their relationship evolved from innocent beginnings in karting circuits to a brotherhood of sorts, as they navigated the challenges of adolescence and early careers together. However, the stakes in Formula 1 are infinitely higher, and the pressures immense. As teammates fighting for the same ultimate prize—the World Championship—their friendship was tested in ways neither could have anticipated. The narrative of their evolving relationship offers valuable insights into human nature, the cost of success, and the intricate dance between personal bonds and professional ambitions.

Purpose and Scope of the Book

This book aims to delve deep into the intricate tapestry of the Hamilton-Rosberg rivalry, exploring not just the events that transpired but the emotions, motivations, and consequences that defined their journey. Through comprehensive analysis and storytelling, we will chart their paths from childhood friends to fierce competitors, examining the factors that fueled their rivalry and the impact it had on their lives and the sport.

The chapters ahead will offer a chronological account of their careers, highlighting key moments that shaped their destinies. We will explore the psychological aspects of their competition, the role of team dynamics at Mercedes, and the broader implications for Formula 1. Interviews, anecdotes, and behind-the-scenes insights will provide a nuanced perspective, shedding light on aspects of their story that are often overlooked.

What Readers Can Expect to Learn and Explore

Readers embarking on this journey can expect to gain a comprehensive understanding of one of Formula 1's most captivating rivalries. The book will:

- **Illuminate the Personal Histories**: Discover how Hamilton's upbringing in Stevenage and Rosberg's heritage as the son of a World Champion influenced their characters and careers.

- **Examine the Evolution of Their Relationship**: Trace the transformation from childhood friends to rivals, understanding the personal and professional factors that contributed to their changing dynamics.

- **Analyze Key Races and Incidents**: Relive the pivotal moments on the track that defined their rivalry, including controversial collisions and strategic battles.

- **Explore Psychological and Team Dynamics**: Delve into the mental aspects of high-level competition and how team politics and management strategies affected their rivalry.

- **Understand the Impact on Formula 1**: Learn about the broader effects their rivalry had on the sport, including technological advancements, changes in team management, and influence on future driver relationships.

- **Reflect on Universal Themes**: Consider the lessons their story offers about ambition, friendship, ethics, and the human spirit's resilience in the face of intense competition.

Ultimately, this book is not just for Formula 1 enthusiasts but for anyone interested in the complexities of human relationships under pressure. It is a study of how two individuals can be driven together and apart by shared goals, how personal history can intensify professional rivalry, and how the pursuit of greatness often comes with profound personal costs.

As we embark on this exploration, we invite readers to look beyond the headlines and race results, to understand the human stories at the core of this modern rivalry. Through their journey, we hope to gain insights into not only the world of Formula 1 but also the broader themes of competition, friendship, and what it means to strive for excellence in the modern era.

Chapter 1: Early Lives and Racing Origins

The story of Lewis Hamilton and Nico Rosberg begins not on the grand stages of Formula 1 circuits, but in the formative years of their childhoods—a time when dreams are untainted by reality, and ambition knows no bounds. Their early lives set the foundation for what would become one of the most intense rivalries in modern motorsport history. Though their paths would eventually converge, their upbringings were as diverse as their driving styles, shaped by different cultures, environments, and familial influences.

Lewis Hamilton's Upbringing

Born on January 7, 1985, in the humble town of Stevenage, Hertfordshire, England, Lewis Carl Davidson Hamilton was a child of mixed heritage in a predominantly white community. His father, Anthony Hamilton, of Grenadian descent, and his mother, Carmen Larbalestier, separated when Lewis was just two years old. Lewis stayed with his mother and half-sisters until the age of twelve before moving in with his father, stepmother Linda, and half-brother Nicolas.

Growing up, Lewis faced the challenges of racial discrimination and the financial constraints of a working-class family. Stevenage, while not impoverished, offered few opportunities for a young black boy with aspirations that stretched beyond the town's borders. Yet, it was here that Lewis's love for speed and competition began to take shape.

At the tender age of six, Lewis received a remote-controlled car from his father. His uncanny ability to master the toy caught Anthony's attention, prompting him to buy Lewis his first go-kart when he was eight years old. The kart was a humble contraption by racing standards, but for Lewis, it was the gateway to a new world. Anthony recognized his son's talent and was determined to nurture it, despite the significant financial burden.

Anthony Hamilton worked multiple jobs—ranging from IT management to vending machine maintenance—to fund Lewis's budding racing career. He often slept in his car during race weekends to save money, all while juggling the responsibilities of supporting his family. Anthony's unwavering commitment was not just about racing; it was about giving his son the chance to excel in a world where opportunities were scarce for someone of his background.

Lewis quickly made a name for himself in the karting circuits. By the age of ten, he had won his first British Karting Championship. It was around this time that a young Lewis approached McLaren team principal Ron Dennis at an awards ceremony, boldly declaring his intention to race for McLaren one day. Impressed by the youngster's confidence, Dennis wrote in his autograph book, "Phone me in nine years, we'll sort something out then." This encounter would prove prophetic, setting the stage for Lewis's meteoric rise in motorsport.

Nico Rosberg's Heritage

In contrast to Lewis's modest beginnings, Nico Erik Rosberg was born into racing royalty on June 27, 1985, in Wiesbaden, Germany. The son of Finnish driver Keke Rosberg—the 1982 Formula 1 World Champion—and his German wife, Gesine Gleitsmann, Nico was introduced to the world of motorsport from birth. However, Keke was determined that his son would not be handed success on a silver platter.

Nico spent his early years in Monaco, a haven for the wealthy and a hub for motorsport enthusiasts. Growing up in such an environment, he was exposed to the glamour and pressures of racing life. Keke, aware of the pitfalls that can accompany fame and privilege, sought to instill in Nico the values of hard work and humility. He refrained from pushing his son into racing, instead allowing Nico to discover his passion organically.

Multilingual and academically gifted, Nico had the world at his feet. He was fluent in German, English, Italian, French, and Spanish, a testament to his international upbringing. Despite the allure of various career paths, the call of motorsport proved irresistible. At the age of six, Nico began karting, quickly showcasing a natural talent that mirrored his father's racing instincts.

Keke played a subtle yet significant role in Nico's development. While he provided guidance and access to resources, he was careful not to overshadow his son's journey. Keke believed that Nico needed to earn his achievements, a philosophy that would shape Nico's approach to racing and competition.

First Steps into Motorsports

For both Lewis and Nico, karting was the crucible in which their racing identities were forged. The karting circuits of Europe are fiercely competitive, often seen as the essential proving ground for future Formula 1 talent. It was in this environment that the two young drivers would eventually meet, but before their paths crossed, each was making waves in their own right.

Lewis's early karting career was marked by a series of impressive victories. By the age of twelve, he had secured multiple championships, including the Super One Series and the Kartmasters British Grand Prix. His aggressive driving style and relentless determination caught the attention of talent scouts and sponsors. In 1998, McLaren and Mercedes-Benz signed Lewis to their Young Driver Support Programme, making him the youngest driver to secure a contract that would support his racing career through the junior ranks.

This partnership was a turning point for the Hamilton family. The financial support alleviated some of the burdens that Anthony had shouldered, allowing Lewis to focus more on honing his skills. Yet, the pressures intensified as expectations grew. Lewis was not just racing for himself but representing a major automotive brand, a responsibility that weighed heavily on his young shoulders.

Meanwhile, Nico was carving his own path through the karting world. Competing in various European championships, he demonstrated a cerebral approach to racing, combining technical precision with strategic thinking. In 2000, he finished third in the European Karting Championship, signaling his readiness to move up the ranks.

Nico's upbringing afforded him certain advantages—access to top-tier equipment, training facilities, and the wisdom of a World Champion father. However, with these advantages came the pressure to live up to the Rosberg name. Nico was acutely aware that he needed to prove himself on merit, not just pedigree.

Both drivers exhibited early signs of the talent and ambition that would define their careers. Their successes in karting led them to the highly competitive world of Formula racing, where their paths would finally intersect. Despite their different backgrounds, they shared a common goal: to reach the pinnacle of motorsport. Little did they know that their journeys, while starting worlds apart, were on a collision course that would alter the trajectory of their lives and the landscape of Formula 1.

The early lives of Lewis Hamilton and Nico Rosberg set the stage for everything that would follow. Their upbringings molded them into the individuals they became—shaped by family influences, personal challenges, and the relentless pursuit of their dreams. Understanding their origins provides crucial insight into the complexities of their later rivalry. It highlights how two young boys, driven by passion and guided by very different circumstances, embarked on paths that would eventually lead them to both camaraderie and conflict on the world's biggest racing platform.

Chapter 2: Karting Days—Where Friendship Began

The winding tracks of European karting circuits have long been the proving grounds for future Formula 1 stars. It was on these serpentine paths of asphalt that Lewis Hamilton and Nico Rosberg first crossed paths, igniting a friendship that would carry them through the formative years of their racing careers. Their meeting was not just a collision of two budding talents but the beginning of a complex relationship that blended camaraderie with competition.

Meeting on the Karting Circuit

In the late 1990s, the European karting scene was a hotbed of young talent, each racer harboring dreams of grandeur. Lewis Hamilton, a tenacious driver from England, and Nico Rosberg, the multilingual prodigy from Monaco, found themselves competing in the same events, their paths inevitably converging.

They first met in 1997 at the age of twelve, during the Junior Monaco Kart Cup. The event was prestigious, attracting the best young karters from around the world. Amidst the buzz and excitement, Lewis and Nico were introduced, two boys from different worlds brought together by their shared passion for speed. Lewis, with his infectious smile and boundless energy, immediately struck a chord with Nico, whose reserved demeanor masked a fierce competitive spirit.

Initial impressions were positive; they recognized in each other a kindred spirit. Both were intensely focused yet still able to enjoy the simple pleasures of youth. They shared laughs, exchanged stories about their races, and found common ground despite their differing backgrounds. Lewis was captivated by Nico's multilingual abilities and worldly experiences, while Nico admired Lewis's raw talent and relentless determination.

Their mutual respect was evident on and off the track. In races, they pushed each other to new heights, each recognizing that the other could bring out their best performances. Off the track, they bonded over typical adolescent interests—football, video games, and a burgeoning fascination with the broader world of motorsport.

Teammates and Friends

Their friendship deepened when they became teammates for Team MBM (Mercedes-Benz McLaren) in 2000. The team was a collaboration between two giants of motorsport, designed to nurture young talent and prepare them for higher echelons of racing. Being selected for such a program was an honor, and for Lewis and Nico, it meant access to superior equipment, coaching, and opportunities.

As teammates, they traveled together across Europe, competing in various karting championships. The shared experiences of long journeys, intense training sessions, and the highs and lows of racing life forged a strong bond between them. They often stayed in the same hotels, ate meals together, and spent countless hours discussing racing strategies, their favorite drivers, and their aspirations.

Their contrasting personalities complemented each other. Lewis's extroverted nature brought a sense of spontaneity and fun, while Nico's analytical approach added depth to their conversations. They learned from each other—Lewis picking up some of Nico's disciplined habits, and Nico embracing a bit of Lewis's flair.

Their families also grew close. Anthony Hamilton and Keke Rosberg, though coming from different backgrounds, shared the common goal of supporting their sons without overshadowing them. The fathers exchanged insights about the sport, sometimes standing together on the sidelines, watching their boys race with pride.

Early Rivalry

Despite their friendship, both Lewis and Nico were fiercely competitive. Karting, while a stepping stone, was no less intense than professional racing. Every race was an opportunity to prove oneself, and neither was willing to concede an inch on the track.

As teammates, they often found themselves battling for the same victories. Their competitive spirit was palpable during races, where overtakes and defensive maneuvers became personal duels. They pushed each other to the limits, each victory hard-fought and each loss a lesson.

One notable battle occurred during the 2000 European Karting Championship. The race was crucial, with scouts and sponsors watching closely. Lewis and Nico started side by side on the grid, both determined to claim the top spot. The race was a masterclass in skill and strategy, with the lead changing multiple times. In the end, Lewis edged out Nico by the slimmest of margins. As they crossed the finish line, the tension dissolved into mutual admiration. They embraced, acknowledging the exceptional effort each had put forth.

Off the track, any lingering frustrations were quickly set aside. They understood that their rivalry was elevating their performances, each serving as the benchmark for the other. This early rivalry laid the groundwork for their future interactions, teaching them how to balance friendship with competition.

Their coaches noted how their relationship was unique. It was rare for two top talents to maintain such a strong friendship amidst intense rivalry. They managed to compartmentalize their competitiveness, ensuring it did not erode the respect and affection they had for one another.

As their karting careers progressed, so did their reputations. They were no longer just promising young drivers; they were emerging as the faces of the next generation in motorsport. Their success caught the attention of major teams and sponsors, setting the stage for their transition into higher levels of racing.

The karting days of Lewis Hamilton and Nico Rosberg were more than just a prelude to their Formula 1 careers; they were the crucible in which their characters were tested and forged. Meeting as young boys with a shared dream, they built a friendship that would endure the pressures of competition—for a time. Their early experiences together, both as teammates and rivals, shaped their understanding of what it means to strive for greatness alongside a friend.

This period was marked by innocence and optimism, a time before the weight of professional expectations would complicate their relationship. They learned valuable lessons about sportsmanship, respect, and the delicate balance required to maintain a friendship in a competitive environment. These lessons would be tested in the years to come, as they moved up the ranks and the stakes grew ever higher.

Their karting days remain a cherished memory for both men—a reminder of where they came from and the pure love of racing that brought them together. It was a time when the thrill of the race was untainted by the complexities of fame and fortune, and when two young drivers could dream freely about conquering the world, side by side.

Chapter 3: Climbing the Ranks—Paths Diverge

As the new millennium unfolded, Lewis Hamilton and Nico Rosberg stood on the cusp of promising careers. Their karting successes had placed them firmly on the radar of talent scouts and team managers across Europe. However, the paths they would take from this point diverged, shaped by personal choices, opportunities, and the relentless pursuit of their individual ambitions. While their ultimate goal remained the same—to reach the pinnacle of motorsport—the routes they navigated were as distinct as their personalities.

Lewis Hamilton's Journey

Progression through Formula Renault and GP2

After dominating the karting scene, Lewis Hamilton made the natural progression to single-seater racing in 2002, joining the Formula Renault UK series. Driving for Manor Motorsport, he faced a steep learning curve, adapting to the increased power and complexity of the vehicles. In his debut season, Lewis finished third overall, a commendable achievement that showcased his adaptability and raw speed.

The following year, he continued in Formula Renault UK, determined to claim the championship. His efforts paid off spectacularly. Lewis won ten out of fifteen races, securing the title with an impressive display of consistency and skill. His performance was a clear message to the motorsport world: a new star was rising.

In 2004, seeking greater challenges, Lewis moved to the Formula 3 Euro Series with Manor Motorsport, though the season proved difficult. Mechanical issues and a lack of familiarity with the circuits hindered his progress. Undeterred, he switched to ASM Formule 3 in 2005, a move that reignited his momentum. Under the guidance of the experienced team, Lewis dominated the series, winning fifteen of the twenty races and clinching the championship.

His success in Formula 3 caught the attention of ART Grand Prix, who offered him a seat in the GP2 Series for 2006. GP2 was the final stepping stone to Formula 1, and Lewis embraced the challenge with characteristic determination. The competition was fierce, featuring talented drivers from around the globe. Lewis rose to the occasion, delivering standout performances that included memorable victories at Silverstone and a stunning double win at the Nürburgring.

The most notable display of his talent came during the Turkish Grand Prix weekend, where he recovered from a spin that left him eighteenth to finish second, overtaking multiple cars with daring and precision. His ability to remain composed under pressure and execute flawless overtakes marked him as a driver of exceptional caliber. Lewis secured the GP2 championship in his rookie year, a feat that solidified his reputation as a future Formula 1 sensation.

Signing with McLaren's Young Driver Program

Lewis's relationship with McLaren dated back to his karting days when he signed with the McLaren and Mercedes-Benz Young Driver Support Programme in 1998. This partnership provided him with financial backing and access to top-tier resources, but it also came with high expectations.

Throughout his ascent, McLaren closely monitored his progress. Ron Dennis, McLaren's team principal, had been instrumental in nurturing Lewis's career, seeing in him the potential to become a world champion. After his triumph in GP2, the question was not if Lewis would join Formula 1, but when and with which team.

In late 2006, McLaren made the pivotal decision to promote Lewis to a race seat for the 2007 Formula 1 season, partnering him with the reigning two-time World Champion, Fernando Alonso. The announcement was met with both excitement and skepticism. While Lewis's talent was undeniable, some questioned whether a rookie driver could handle the pressures of Formula 1, especially alongside a driver of Alonso's stature.

Lewis embraced the opportunity with humility and confidence. He knew that his journey had been a culmination of years of hard work, sacrifices made by himself and his family, and the unwavering support of those who believed in him. Stepping into Formula 1 was not just a personal achievement; it was a milestone that resonated with many who saw in Lewis a trailblazer breaking barriers in a sport not known for its diversity.

Nico Rosberg's Ascendancy

Success in Formula BMW and GP2

While Lewis was making waves in the UK, Nico Rosberg was forging his own path through the European racing circuits. In 2002, he competed in the Formula BMW ADAC championship with VIVA Racing. Demonstrating his technical acumen and consistent performance, Nico dominated the series, winning nine out of twenty races and securing the championship title.

His success in Formula BMW opened doors to higher categories. In 2003, Nico progressed to the Formula 3 Euro Series with Team Rosberg, managed by his father. The move was challenging; the competition was tougher, and the learning curve steeper. Over two seasons, Nico honed his skills, achieving several podiums but no wins. Recognizing the need for a change, he joined ART Grand Prix for the inaugural GP2 Series in 2005.

Driving for ART, Nico found a new stride. The GP2 car suited his precise driving style, and he quickly adapted to the strategic nuances of the series. He engaged in fierce battles with competitors, showcasing not only speed but also tactical intelligence. Nico's ability to manage tires, fuel loads, and race pace set him apart.

In a dramatic season finale at Bahrain, Nico clinched the GP2 championship, making history as the series' first champion. His victory was a testament to his perseverance and growth as a driver. It also positioned him as a prime candidate for a Formula 1 seat.

Entry into Formula 1 with Williams

Nico's GP2 success did not go unnoticed. Williams F1 Team, one of the sport's storied outfits, offered him a race seat for the 2006 season. The opportunity was significant; Williams had a legacy of nurturing young talent, and Nico was eager to make his mark.

Debuting at the Bahrain Grand Prix, Nico made an immediate impact. He set the fastest lap of the race—the youngest driver ever to do so at the time—and finished in a respectable seventh place, earning his first two championship points. His performance signaled that he was more than ready for Formula 1's demands.

The subsequent seasons with Williams were a mix of challenges and achievements. The team was grappling with performance issues, and the car was often uncompetitive compared to the frontrunners. Despite this, Nico extracted the maximum from his machinery, earning podium finishes and consistently outperforming more experienced teammates.

Nico's time at Williams was characterized by steady growth. He developed a reputation for technical feedback and a methodical approach to racing. His engineering background—having studied aeronautical engineering briefly at Imperial College London—allowed him to contribute significantly to car development.

By the end of the 2009 season, Nico had established himself as a reliable and talented driver. However, it was clear that to achieve his ambitions of winning races and championships, a move to a more competitive team was necessary.

Contrasting Experiences

Differences in Opportunities and Challenges

Lewis and Nico's journeys to Formula 1, while both successful, were marked by contrasting experiences shaped by their backgrounds and the opportunities available to them.

Lewis's partnership with McLaren provided him with a direct pipeline to a top-tier Formula 1 team. The support he received was instrumental in overcoming financial barriers and accessing resources that might have otherwise been out of reach. However, this also placed him under intense scrutiny. The expectations were immense; he was not only representing himself but also the McLaren brand and the hopes of those who saw him as a pioneer.

Nico, on the other hand, navigated his career with the guidance of his father but without the backing of a manufacturer team during his early Formula 1 years. His time at Williams was both a blessing and a challenge. While he gained valuable experience and demonstrated his capabilities, the team's struggles limited his ability to fight at the front of the grid.

Their differing paths highlight the nuances of motorsport careers. Access to competitive machinery, financial support, and team dynamics play crucial roles in a driver's success. Both faced pressures unique to their situations—Lewis with the weight of expectation and media attention, Nico with the task of proving himself independently of his father's legacy.

How Their Early Careers Shaped Them

The experiences of their early careers profoundly influenced Lewis and Nico, both as drivers and individuals.

For Lewis, the rapid ascent to Formula 1 and immediate success reinforced his belief in his abilities. His rookie season in 2007 was nothing short of sensational, nearly winning the World Championship. This early triumph set a high bar for his future performance and instilled a confidence that would become a hallmark of his racing style.

However, the pressures of being in the spotlight also taught Lewis valuable lessons about resilience and focus.

Navigating the complexities of team politics, media scrutiny, and the demands of top-level competition required maturity beyond his years. These challenges contributed to his development as a mentally strong and adaptable driver.

Nico's journey instilled in him a different set of qualities. His time at Williams, often fighting in the midfield, taught him patience and the importance of technical proficiency. He learned how to maximize limited resources and the value of consistent performance. These attributes would later serve him well when he joined Mercedes, a team with championship aspirations.

Moreover, Nico's determination to forge his own identity, separate from his father's achievements, fueled his work ethic. He was meticulous in his preparations, dedicated to fitness, and keenly involved in the technical aspects of racing. This approach would become a key factor in his ability to challenge the best in the sport.

Their divergent paths also affected their perspectives on competition and success. Lewis, accustomed to winning from an early age, approached races with an aggressive confidence. Nico, having faced more constraints, developed a strategic mindset, often playing the long game in pursuit of his goals.

As Lewis Hamilton and Nico Rosberg climbed the ranks of motorsport, their paths reflected the diverse nature of the journey to Formula 1. Their experiences, while different, equipped them with the skills, knowledge, and character traits that would define their professional relationships and rivalries in the years to come.

Their individual stories during this period are a testament to the multifaceted challenges faced by aspiring drivers. Talent alone is not enough; navigating the complexities of sponsorship, team politics, and personal development are equally critical. For Lewis and Nico, every victory and setback along the way shaped their destinies, setting the stage for their eventual reunion as teammates at Mercedes.

The divergence of their paths during these formative years added layers to their relationship. Each brought unique experiences and perspectives to the table, which would influence how they interacted as teammates and competitors. Understanding their journeys provides essential context for the dynamics that would later unfold—a blend of friendship, rivalry, and the relentless pursuit of greatness that would captivate the world of Formula 1.

Chapter 4: Early Formula 1 Careers

The ascent to Formula 1 represents the culmination of years of dedication, sacrifice, and unrelenting ambition. For Lewis Hamilton and Nico Rosberg, entering the highest echelon of motorsport was both a dream realized and the beginning of a new set of challenges. Their early years in Formula 1 would see them navigate different trajectories—Hamilton bursting onto the scene with immediate impact, and Rosberg methodically building his reputation in a mid-field team. As they settled into the sport, their paths occasionally crossed on the track, foreshadowing the intense rivalry that would later define their careers.

Hamilton at McLaren (2007–2012)

Immediate Impact and Rookie Records

When Lewis Hamilton made his Formula 1 debut with McLaren in 2007, he did so under intense scrutiny and sky-high expectations. Partnered with Fernando Alonso, the reigning two-time World Champion, Lewis was thrust into the spotlight. Many wondered if the young rookie could handle the pressure of competing at the pinnacle of motorsport alongside one of its greatest talents.

From the very first race in Australia, Lewis dispelled any doubts about his readiness. He finished third, achieving a podium on debut—a rare feat in Formula 1. His performance was characterized by a fearless overtaking maneuver at the start, where he boldly passed his seasoned teammate and other competitors. This audacious move set the tone for his rookie season.

Lewis continued to impress throughout the early part of the season. In the next four races, he finished second each time, demonstrating remarkable consistency. Then, at the Canadian Grand Prix, he secured his maiden victory, leading from pole position and managing the race with the composure of a veteran. This win made him the first black driver to win a Formula 1 race, a historic moment that resonated far beyond the sport.

He followed up with another victory at the United States Grand Prix, solidifying his status as a championship contender. By mid-season, Lewis was leading the drivers' standings, a remarkable achievement for a rookie. His aggressive yet controlled driving style, coupled with his ability to extract maximum performance from the car, set several rookie records. He became the youngest driver to lead the World Championship and the first to finish on the podium in his first nine races.

However, the season was not without its challenges. Tensions within McLaren escalated as Lewis and Alonso vied for supremacy. The rivalry between teammates culminated in several controversial incidents, including a qualifying dispute at the Hungarian Grand Prix that resulted in internal penalties. The strain affected team dynamics and ultimately had repercussions on the championship outcome.

The season finale in Brazil was a dramatic showdown between Lewis, Alonso, and Ferrari's Kimi Räikkönen. A gearbox issue at the start dropped Lewis down the order, and despite a valiant effort to recover, he finished seventh. Räikkönen won the race and the championship by a single point, leaving Lewis and Alonso tied for second place. It was a bitter end to an otherwise phenomenal debut season for Lewis.

2008 World Championship Victory

Undeterred by the previous year's disappointment, Lewis entered the 2008 season with renewed determination. McLaren had resolved internal conflicts, and Lewis was now the clear number one driver following Alonso's departure. The season was fiercely competitive, with challenges from Ferrari's Felipe Massa and BMW Sauber's Robert Kubica.

Lewis began the season strongly, winning the opening race in Australia. However, inconsistency and a series of penalties, including a significant one at the Belgian Grand Prix for cutting a chicane, threatened his championship aspirations. The battle with Massa intensified as the season progressed, with both drivers exchanging the lead in the standings.

The championship fight culminated in one of the most dramatic conclusions in Formula 1 history at the Brazilian Grand Prix. Lewis entered the race seven points ahead of Massa. In changing weather conditions, strategy calls became critical. On the final lap, Lewis was running in sixth place, which would have handed the title to Massa, who had won the race. In a stunning turn of events, Lewis overtook Toyota's Timo Glock in the final corners to reclaim fifth place, securing the championship by a single point.

At 23 years old, Lewis became the youngest World Champion at the time. His victory was celebrated globally, marking a significant milestone not only for him personally but also for diversity in motorsport. The triumph was a testament to his resilience, talent, and the ability to perform under immense pressure.

Over the next several years with McLaren, Lewis experienced a mix of successes and setbacks. The team faced challenges with car development, and reliability issues hampered their competitiveness. Despite this, Lewis continued to win races and set records. In 2010, he remained in contention for the championship until the penultimate race, showcasing his persistent competitiveness.

By 2012, frustrations with McLaren's inconsistencies and strategic errors led Lewis to consider new opportunities. His tenure with the team that had nurtured his career from adolescence was coming to a natural conclusion. The decision to leave was not taken lightly, but a new chapter beckoned.

Rosberg at Williams (2006–2009)

Development Years in a Mid-Field Team

Nico Rosberg's entry into Formula 1 with Williams in 2006 marked the beginning of a steady climb up the motorsport ladder. Unlike Hamilton, who debuted with a top team, Nico started with a team that was rebuilding and facing technical challenges. Williams had a storied history but was struggling to return to its former glory.

In his debut race in Bahrain, Nico showcased his potential by setting the fastest lap and finishing seventh, earning two championship points. His performance was a bright spot in an otherwise challenging season for Williams, who grappled with reliability issues and lack of pace. Nico's technical feedback and analytical approach were highly valued by the team, contributing to car development.

The 2007 season saw some improvements, but Williams remained a mid-field contender at best. Nico consistently outperformed his teammate, demonstrating his ability to maximize the car's potential. His driving was characterized by precision and a strong understanding of race strategy.

In 2008, the team switched to Toyota engines, which brought some progress. The season opener in Australia was a breakthrough for Nico, where he achieved his first Formula 1 podium by finishing third. It was a moment of vindication for his perseverance. Throughout the season, he continued to deliver solid performances, though the car's limitations prevented regular podium finishes.

The 2009 season brought significant regulation changes aimed at improving overtaking and leveling the competitive field. Williams started the season strongly, with Nico frequently setting fast lap times in practice sessions. However, the team struggled to convert this speed into race results. Despite the challenges, Nico finished in the points on several occasions and consistently outperformed his teammate.

First Podiums and Standout Performances

Nico's tenure at Williams was marked by flashes of brilliance amidst a backdrop of mediocrity. His podium in Australia was followed by another at the 2008 Singapore Grand Prix, Formula 1's first night race. Despite a penalty that threatened his race, Nico drove superbly to finish second, showcasing his ability to capitalize on chaotic conditions.

His performances did not go unnoticed. Paddock insiders praised his professionalism and technical aptitude. He was often linked with moves to more competitive teams, but contractual obligations and market dynamics kept him at Williams. Nonetheless, these years were instrumental in shaping Nico as a driver who combined speed with intelligence.

Nico's time at Williams honed his racecraft. Operating without the pressure of championship expectations allowed him to develop at his own pace. He became adept at tire management, fuel conservation, and strategic overtaking—skills that would prove invaluable in the future.

By the end of 2009, it was evident that Williams could not provide Nico with the machinery to fight for wins consistently. Seeking new horizons, he began exploring options with other teams. The stage was set for the next phase of his career.

Parallel Progressions

Observations of Each Other's Careers

Throughout these formative years in Formula 1, Lewis and Nico kept a close eye on each other's progress. Their shared history and friendship meant that they remained interested in one another's fortunes, even as their careers took different trajectories.

Lewis's immediate success was a source of admiration and perhaps a touch of envy for Nico. He recognized the advantages of being in a top team but also respected the pressure that came with it. Nico was pleased for his friend but was also motivated to elevate his own performance.

Conversely, Lewis was aware of Nico's efforts at Williams. He understood the challenges of driving for a team that was not at the front of the grid. Lewis appreciated Nico's perseverance and his ability to extract the best from his car. They occasionally exchanged messages of encouragement, maintaining a cordial relationship despite the competitive environment.

Their paths would cross on the track, but direct battles were infrequent due to the performance gap between their teams. When they did compete wheel-to-wheel, it was often in changing conditions or during strategic phases of a race. These encounters were marked by mutual respect and clean racing.

Occasional On-Track Encounters

One notable on-track battle occurred during the 2008 Australian Grand Prix. With both drivers in strong positions, they found themselves vying for the podium. The duel was intense but fair, each driver giving the other space while pushing to the limit. Lewis ultimately finished first, with Nico securing third—the first time both stood on the podium together in Formula 1.

Another memorable encounter was at the 2009 Japanese Grand Prix. In a race affected by inclement weather and strategic pit stops, Lewis and Nico found themselves racing closely. Nico's strategic gamble on tire choice paid off, allowing him to finish ahead of Lewis, who was struggling with his car's setup.

These moments were glimpses of what could be possible if they were competing in equally matched machinery. The prospect of being teammates again began to surface in media speculation, especially with the impending return of Mercedes as a full works team.

The early Formula 1 careers of Lewis Hamilton and Nico Rosberg were characterized by divergent paths that reflected their unique circumstances. Lewis's rapid rise to the top with McLaren showcased his extraordinary talent and ability to handle pressure. His World Championship victory in 2008 solidified his status as one of the sport's elite drivers.

Nico's steady development at Williams demonstrated his resilience and technical prowess. While he lacked the equipment to fight at the front consistently, his performances earned him respect and positioned him as a sought-after talent for teams looking to strengthen their driver lineup.

Their parallel progressions set the stage for future collaboration and conflict. As both drivers sought new opportunities to achieve their ambitions, the possibility of reuniting became increasingly tangible. Their early careers had shaped them into formidable competitors, each with a distinct approach to racing. The foundations were laid for the next chapter of their intertwined stories—a chapter that would see them become teammates once more, this time under the banner of Mercedes, where their rivalry would reach unprecedented heights.

Chapter 5: Reuniting at Mercedes—Teammates Again

The world of Formula 1 is a constantly evolving tapestry of teams rising and falling, drivers shifting alliances, and technology pushing the boundaries of speed and performance. Amidst this ever-changing landscape, the paths of Lewis Hamilton and Nico Rosberg were set to converge once more. The reunion at Mercedes not only rekindled their childhood friendship but also set the stage for one of the most intense rivalries in the sport's history. To understand the significance of their reunion, it is essential to delve into the resurgence of the Mercedes team and the circumstances that brought these two formidable talents together under one banner.

Mercedes' Return to Formula 1

The Team's History and Ambitions

Mercedes-Benz has a storied legacy in motorsport, with roots stretching back to the very inception of Grand Prix racing. In the 1930s, the "Silver Arrows" dominated the European racing scene, establishing a reputation for engineering excellence and competitive prowess. However, the tragedies of motorsport in the mid-20th century, including the catastrophic 1955 Le Mans disaster involving a Mercedes car, led the company to withdraw from racing activities.

Decades later, Mercedes gradually re-entered motorsport, initially supplying engines and forming partnerships with existing teams. Their collaboration with McLaren yielded significant success, including multiple World Championships with drivers like Mika Häkkinen and Lewis

Hamilton himself. Despite these achievements, Mercedes aspired to re-establish itself as a full works team, controlling both chassis and engine development to compete at the highest level.

In 2009, an opportunity arose when Brawn GP, a team that had remarkably won both the Constructors' and Drivers' Championships in its debut season, became available for purchase. Mercedes seized the moment, acquiring a 75.1% stake in Brawn GP and rebranding it as Mercedes GP Petronas Formula One Team for the 2010 season. This move signaled Mercedes' serious intent to reclaim its former glory in Formula 1.

The team enlisted the expertise of Ross Brawn, a master strategist and technical director renowned for his success with Ferrari and his namesake team, Brawn GP. They also secured the talents of Nico Rosberg and the legendary Michael Schumacher, who came out of retirement to join the project. The combination of seasoned leadership and driving talent set high expectations, but the initial seasons proved challenging.

From 2010 to 2012, Mercedes grappled with the complexities of modern Formula 1. The team managed to secure occasional podiums and a solitary victory at the 2012 Chinese Grand Prix with Nico Rosberg, but consistency eluded them. Recognizing the need for further evolution, Mercedes embarked on a strategic overhaul. Key to this was attracting top engineering talent and reassessing their driver lineup to position themselves for future success.

The impending regulatory changes for the 2014 season, which included the introduction of new hybrid power units, presented an opportunity. Mercedes, with its extensive resources and engineering expertise, aimed to capitalize on these changes to leapfrog established frontrunners. The team set ambitious goals: to become a dominant force in Formula 1 and to win both the Constructors' and Drivers' Championships.

Hamilton Joins Rosberg at Mercedes (2013)

Circumstances of Hamilton's Move

By the end of 2012, Lewis Hamilton found himself at a crossroads. Despite his deep ties to McLaren, the team that had nurtured his career since adolescence, Lewis was growing increasingly frustrated. McLaren had struggled with reliability issues and strategic errors that cost him valuable points and potential victories. The relationship was strained further by contractual disputes and disagreements over personal branding and sponsorship rights.

Meanwhile, Mercedes courted Lewis with a compelling proposition. Ross Brawn and team principal Toto Wolff presented a vision of a team on the rise, one that would center around Lewis as their leading driver. They offered not just a competitive salary but also the freedom to develop his personal brand and the opportunity to be part of building something significant from the ground up.

The allure of reuniting with his old friend Nico Rosberg was an additional incentive. Lewis saw the potential for a positive partnership that could push both drivers to new heights. Moreover, the chance to work with Ross Brawn and the engineering team at Mercedes appealed to his desire for technical involvement and innovation.

After careful deliberation, Lewis made the bold decision to leave McLaren and sign a three-year contract with Mercedes starting in the 2013 season. The move was met with surprise and skepticism. Many questioned why a World Champion would leave an established top team for one that had yet to prove itself as a consistent frontrunner.

Expectations and Media Reactions

The announcement of Lewis Hamilton joining Mercedes sent shockwaves through the Formula 1 community. Media outlets buzzed with speculation and analysis. Critics argued that Lewis was taking a significant risk, potentially sacrificing immediate competitiveness for uncertain future gains. Pundits dubbed it a "gamble," pointing out that Mercedes had only one win since their return as a works team.

Some speculated that the move was motivated by financial gain, while others suggested that Lewis sought a new challenge after years at McLaren. The British press, in particular, expressed mixed feelings. There was disappointment at losing a homegrown talent from a British team but also intrigue at the prospects of his new venture.

Supporters of the move highlighted Mercedes' substantial investment in technology and personnel. They noted the recruitment of key figures like Aldo Costa from Ferrari and Geoff Willis from Red Bull Racing, indicating the team's commitment to excellence. The upcoming regulatory changes were also seen as a potential equalizer, giving Mercedes an opportunity to leap ahead.

Lewis himself remained confident and composed in the face of scrutiny. In interviews, he emphasized his belief in Mercedes' vision and his excitement about contributing to the team's growth. He acknowledged the challenges but expressed optimism about what they could achieve together.

For Nico Rosberg, the news was both thrilling and professionally significant. Having a driver of Lewis's caliber join the team validated Mercedes' ambitions. It also meant reuniting with his childhood friend and former teammate, adding a personal dimension to the professional relationship.

Renewed Friendship

Initial Camaraderie and Collaboration

As the 2013 season approached, Lewis Hamilton and Nico Rosberg found themselves teammates once more, this time on the grand stage of Formula 1. The reunion rekindled memories of their karting days, evoking a sense of nostalgia and camaraderie. They were no longer the wide-eyed boys dreaming of the big leagues; they were accomplished drivers ready to take on new challenges together.

In the early days of their partnership at Mercedes, the atmosphere was positive and collaborative. Both drivers were committed to helping the team progress and were open in sharing data and insights. They worked closely during testing sessions, providing feedback to engineers and participating in technical briefings. Their personal rapport eased communication, fostering a productive environment.

Off the track, Lewis and Nico often spent time together, continuing the friendship that had begun years before. They shared meals, engaged in friendly competitions in activities like golf and table tennis, and occasionally appeared together in media events and promotional activities. Their interactions were marked by mutual respect and a shared sense of purpose.

Team management encouraged this harmony, recognizing the benefits of a united front. Ross Brawn and Toto Wolff emphasized the importance of teamwork and collective effort. They were mindful of potential rivalries but believed that the drivers' history and friendship would contribute positively to the team's dynamics.

Shared Goals for Team Success

Both Lewis and Nico were acutely aware that Mercedes was in a building phase. The team's performance in previous seasons had been inconsistent, and there was work to be done to challenge the established leaders like Red Bull Racing and Ferrari. The drivers embraced this challenge, setting shared goals for team success.

Their primary objective was to help Mercedes secure race wins and establish itself as a regular podium contender. They participated actively in car development, offering detailed feedback on handling, aerodynamics, and power unit performance. Their different driving styles provided valuable data, allowing engineers to create a more versatile and competitive car.

In races, Lewis and Nico demonstrated strategic cooperation. They adhered to team orders when necessary and avoided unnecessary risks when battling each other on the track. Their focus was on maximizing points for the team, recognizing that collective success would benefit them individually in the long run.

The 2013 season saw improvements in Mercedes' performance. The team secured several pole positions and race victories—Nico winning in Monaco and Lewis triumphing in Hungary. These successes were milestones, indicating that Mercedes was moving in the right direction. The drivers celebrated each other's achievements, reinforcing the positive team spirit.

Their collaboration extended beyond the technical aspects. Lewis and Nico engaged in promotional activities to elevate Mercedes' brand presence. They participated in fan events, sponsor engagements, and media appearances, often together. Their chemistry was evident, and they became popular figures, enhancing the team's public image.

The reunion of Lewis Hamilton and Nico Rosberg at Mercedes marked a significant chapter in both their careers. It was a period of renewed friendship, shared ambitions, and collaborative efforts to propel their team to the forefront of Formula 1. The initial camaraderie set a strong foundation, fostering an environment where both drivers could thrive.

However, beneath the surface, the seeds of future rivalry were quietly taking root. As the team's competitiveness increased, so did the stakes. The desire to win, inherent in both drivers, would eventually bring their friendship and professional relationship into sharp focus. But for now, the story was one of unity and optimism, a testament to what could be achieved when talent, ambition, and collaboration converge.

Their journey together at Mercedes was just beginning, and the world watched with anticipation. The stage was set for a new era in Formula 1, one that would test the limits of friendship and competition in ways neither Lewis nor Nico could have fully anticipated. The chapters that followed would chronicle a complex interplay of personal dynamics and professional rivalry, shaping their legacies and leaving an indelible mark on the sport they both loved.

Chapter 6: The 2013 Season—Setting the Stage

The 2013 Formula 1 season was a pivotal moment for both Lewis Hamilton and Nico Rosberg. As they embarked on their first year as teammates at Mercedes, the dynamics within the team and between the drivers began to take shape. This season would lay the groundwork for the events that followed, setting the stage for a rivalry that would captivate the motorsport world. It was a year of adaptation, collaboration, and subtle undercurrents of competition that hinted at the complexities to come.

Team Dynamics

Adapting to New Roles as Teammates

Stepping into the 2013 season, Lewis Hamilton faced the task of integrating into a new team environment after years with McLaren. Mercedes, while familiar in terms of engine partnership, presented a different culture and operational structure. Lewis needed to build relationships with new engineers, mechanics, and team personnel. His arrival also meant adjusting to the working style of Nico Rosberg, who was already established within the team.

Nico, on his part, was entering his fourth season with Mercedes. He had been instrumental in the team's development and had built strong ties within the organization. The arrival of Lewis brought both excitement and uncertainty. While they shared a history of friendship, the dynamics of being teammates in a highly competitive environment required careful navigation.

The initial phase was marked by mutual respect and open communication. Both drivers participated in team-building activities and engaged in collaborative discussions about car development. They shared feedback openly during testing sessions, recognizing that their combined efforts were crucial for the team's progress. The technical staff appreciated their input, noting that their different driving styles provided comprehensive data for optimizing the car's performance.

Adapting to their new roles also involved understanding each other's working methods. Lewis was known for his instinctive driving and ability to find pace in challenging conditions. Nico was meticulous, often delving deep into data analysis and setup adjustments. They learned to appreciate these differences, finding ways to complement each other for the benefit of the team.

However, underlying this collaboration was the awareness that both drivers were competitors with individual ambitions. Balancing personal goals with team objectives required a delicate approach. They needed to establish boundaries that allowed for healthy competition without undermining the team's cohesion.

Balancing Cooperation and Competition

As the season progressed, the balance between cooperation and competition became more nuanced. On one hand, Lewis and Nico continued to work together in technical briefings and strategy sessions. They recognized that improving the car's performance was a collective endeavor, especially as Mercedes sought to challenge the dominance of teams like Red Bull Racing.

On the other hand, the natural competitiveness inherent in both drivers began to surface. Each wanted to assert themselves as the team's leading driver, a position that could influence future development directions and strategic decisions. Friendly banter occasionally gave way to subtle one-upmanship, whether in setting faster lap times during practice or vying for the upper hand in qualifying sessions.

Team management played a crucial role in maintaining harmony. Ross Brawn emphasized the importance of equal treatment and transparency. Both drivers had access to the same equipment and information, and the team avoided favoring one over the other. This approach was intended to foster fair competition while keeping the team's interests paramount.

Despite these efforts, the inherent tension of competing for the same goals began to test their relationship. Instances arose where strategic differences led to disagreements. For example, preferences for tire choices or race strategies sometimes conflicted, requiring mediation from the team. These situations were handled professionally, but they hinted at the potential for deeper conflicts.

Off the track, Lewis and Nico continued to socialize, but the frequency of their interactions decreased as the season wore on. The demands of the championship, combined with their individual focus on performance, left less time for camaraderie. The friendship was still present, but it was gradually being overshadowed by the realities of their competitive environment.

Key Races and Moments

First Wins and Podiums for Mercedes

The 2013 season marked significant milestones for Mercedes, with both Lewis and Nico contributing to the team's ascent. Early in the season, the team demonstrated improved pace, securing strong qualifying positions. However, translating this into race results was initially challenging due to tire degradation issues and race pace discrepancies.

The breakthrough came at the Monaco Grand Prix. Nico Rosberg, starting from pole position, delivered a masterful performance on the tight and unforgiving streets of Monte Carlo. Controlling the race from start to finish, he secured his second career victory and the first win of the season for Mercedes. The triumph was particularly poignant for Nico, whose father Keke Rosberg had won the same race 30 years prior. The victory boosted team morale and validated the progress made in car development.

Lewis Hamilton also made significant contributions. At the Hungarian Grand Prix, he achieved his first win with Mercedes. Starting from pole position, Lewis showcased his exceptional skill in managing tires and maintaining consistent lap times. The victory was a personal milestone, affirming his decision to join Mercedes and demonstrating the team's potential. It was a moment of celebration, with both drivers and team members acknowledging the collective effort involved.

Throughout the season, Mercedes secured multiple podium finishes. The team's competitiveness was evident in qualifying, with numerous front-row starts. However, race pace remained an area for improvement. Both drivers worked closely with engineers to address these challenges, focusing on tire management and aerodynamic efficiency.

These successes signaled Mercedes' emergence as a genuine contender. The victories were not only important for the championship standings but also for establishing the team as a force to be reckoned with. The achievements fueled ambition and set higher expectations for future performances.

Early Signs of Rivalry

Amidst the celebrations and collaborative efforts, subtle signs of rivalry began to emerge between Lewis and Nico. While their interactions remained professional, moments of competitive tension became more frequent.

One of the earliest indications occurred during the Malaysian Grand Prix. In the closing stages of the race, Nico, running in fourth place, was faster than Lewis in third. He requested permission to overtake, believing he could challenge the cars ahead. The team issued orders for both drivers to hold their positions, prioritizing the overall result and preserving the cars. Nico complied, but his frustration was evident over team radio communications.

After the race, Nico expressed his disappointment but maintained that he respected the team's decision. Lewis, acknowledging that Nico had been faster, publicly thanked his teammate for adhering to the team orders. The incident highlighted the delicate balance between individual ambition and team directives. It also underscored the potential for conflict when personal goals intersected with team strategies.

Another moment came during the British Grand Prix at Silverstone. Lewis secured pole position but suffered a tire failure during the race, dropping him down the order. Nico capitalized on the situation, ultimately winning the race. While the victory was a triumph for the team, it also shifted the internal dynamics. Nico's win narrowed the gap between the drivers in the championship standings, intensifying the competitive atmosphere.

Qualifying sessions became arenas for psychological battles. Both drivers pushed the limits, seeking to outpace each other and gain strategic advantages for the races. The margins were often razor-thin, reflecting their closely matched abilities and determination. Media coverage began to focus on this emerging intra-team competition, adding external pressure.

Off-track, the friendly interactions became less frequent. Media obligations, personal commitments, and the increasing focus on performance limited their social engagements. While they remained cordial, the depth of their friendship was tested by the demands of competing at the highest level.

Team management observed these developments with cautious attention. Ross Brawn and Toto Wolff recognized the importance of managing the drivers' relationship to prevent it from affecting team performance. They held meetings to address concerns, reinforcing the principles of mutual respect and team unity.

The 2013 season was a transformative period for Lewis Hamilton, Nico Rosberg, and the Mercedes team. It was a year of significant achievements that set new benchmarks and raised expectations. The drivers adapted to their roles as teammates, navigating the complexities of collaboration and competition. The successes they shared were milestones that validated their efforts and the strategic direction of the team.

However, the early signs of rivalry hinted at the challenges that lay ahead. The subtle shifts in dynamics foreshadowed a more intense competition that would test their friendship and professional relationship. The balance between cooperation and personal ambition became increasingly precarious, setting the stage for the heightened tensions of subsequent seasons.

The foundation laid in 2013 was both promising and fragile. Mercedes had established itself as a contender, and the drivers had demonstrated their capabilities. The stage was set for the team to challenge for championships. Yet, the very elements that fueled their success—the drivers' talent, determination, and competitiveness—also harbored the potential for conflict.

As the sport prepared for significant regulatory changes in 2014, the anticipation grew. The introduction of new hybrid power units and aerodynamic regulations promised to reshape the competitive landscape. Mercedes, investing heavily in these developments, stood on the brink of a new era.

For Lewis and Nico, the journey was about to enter a more complex phase. The convergence of personal ambitions, team objectives, and evolving relationships would create a narrative rich with drama and intrigue. The events of 2013 had set the stage—a prelude to a rivalry that would captivate audiences and leave an indelible mark on Formula 1 history.

Chapter 7: The 2014 Season—Rivalry Ignites

The 2014 Formula 1 season marked a watershed moment in the careers of Lewis Hamilton and Nico Rosberg, as well as in the sport itself. Significant regulation changes reshaped the competitive landscape, propelling Mercedes to the forefront of the grid. With a dominant car beneath them, Lewis and Nico found themselves in a direct battle for the World Championship. What began as a friendly competition between teammates evolved into an intense rivalry, igniting tensions that would test the limits of their friendship and professionalism.

Regulation Changes and Mercedes Dominance

Introduction of Hybrid Engines

The 2014 season ushered in one of the most substantial technical overhauls in Formula 1 history. The sport transitioned from the naturally aspirated 2.4-liter V8 engines to 1.6-liter V6 turbocharged hybrid power units. These new engines featured advanced energy recovery systems (ERS), combining kinetic and thermal energy harvesting to deliver increased efficiency and performance. The changes were aimed at promoting technological innovation and aligning the sport with the automotive industry's shift toward hybrid technology.

The new regulations posed significant challenges for teams and manufacturers. Designing a reliable and powerful hybrid power unit required substantial investment in research and development. Teams had to integrate complex electrical systems with traditional combustion engines, manage heat dissipation, and ensure reliability over long race distances. The learning curve was steep, and not all teams were equally prepared.

Mercedes' Technical Advantage

Mercedes had anticipated the regulatory shift and invested heavily in developing their hybrid power unit, the PU106A Hybrid. Their foresight and resources paid dividends. The Mercedes engine proved to be the most powerful and reliable on the grid, delivering a significant advantage over rival teams. The combination of a potent power unit and an aerodynamically efficient chassis designed by a talented technical team, including Paddy Lowe and Aldo Costa, positioned Mercedes as the team to beat.

The W05 Hybrid, Mercedes' 2014 car, was a masterpiece of engineering. It seamlessly integrated the complex hybrid systems, achieving optimal balance between power and efficiency. The car excelled in both qualifying and race conditions, displaying superior speed on straights and stability through corners. Competitors struggled to match its performance, often lagging by significant margins in lap times.

This technical superiority set the stage for a dominant season. Mercedes secured pole position in all but one race and won 16 out of 19 Grands Prix. The team's advantage was so pronounced that the primary competition often came from within—the battle between Lewis Hamilton and Nico Rosberg became the focal point of the championship narrative.

Championship Battle Begins

Neck-and-Neck Races

From the season opener in Australia, it was clear that the fight for the World Championship would be a duel between the Mercedes drivers. Nico Rosberg claimed victory in Melbourne after Lewis Hamilton retired due to an engine misfire. The early lead gave Nico momentum, but Lewis responded with a series of four consecutive wins in Malaysia, Bahrain, China, and Spain. The two drivers exchanged victories throughout the season, with the championship lead oscillating between them.

The Bahrain Grand Prix was a particularly thrilling showcase of their rivalry. The race featured a fierce, wheel-to-wheel battle between Lewis and Nico, culminating in a nail-biting finish. Despite multiple overtaking attempts by Nico, Lewis defended his position with masterful skill, ultimately securing the win. The duel was praised for its intensity and respectfulness, highlighting the competitive spirit between the teammates.

In Monaco, Nico regained the championship lead with a victory, while Lewis finished second. The pattern of alternating successes continued, keeping the points gap minimal. Both drivers pushed themselves and each other to the limits, extracting every ounce of performance from their cars.

The tension escalated at the Hungarian Grand Prix, where team orders came into play. Lewis, recovering from a pit lane start due to a qualifying fire, was instructed to let Nico pass during the race. Believing it would compromise his own strategy, Lewis refused, resulting in a terse exchange over team radio. The incident underscored the mounting pressures and the complexities of managing two championship contenders within the same team.

Notable Incidents

Monaco Qualifying Controversy

The Monaco Grand Prix, held on the narrow and treacherous streets of Monte Carlo, is a race where qualifying positions are crucial due to the difficulty of overtaking. During the final moments of the qualifying session, Nico Rosberg was on provisional pole with Lewis Hamilton close behind on a faster lap. As Nico approached the Mirabeau corner, he locked up his brakes and went down the escape road, bringing out yellow flags. This incident forced Lewis and other drivers to abort their flying laps, cementing Nico's pole position.

The timing and nature of Nico's off-track excursion raised eyebrows. Speculation arose that the incident was deliberate, aimed at preventing Lewis from taking pole. Lewis, visibly frustrated, hinted at his suspicions in post-session interviews, stating he would "take a page out of [Nico's] book" in future qualifying sessions. The media seized upon the controversy, fueling debates about sportsmanship and integrity.

An investigation by the stewards cleared Nico of any wrongdoing, ruling the incident as a driver error without malicious intent. However, the seeds of mistrust had been sown. The event strained the relationship between the teammates, introducing an element of suspicion that would linger throughout the season.

Belgian Grand Prix Collision

The simmering tensions boiled over at the Belgian Grand Prix in Spa-Francorchamps. On the second lap of the race, Nico attempted to overtake Lewis on the outside heading into Les Combes. As they navigated the corner, their cars made contact—Nico's front wing clipped Lewis's left rear tire, causing a puncture. Lewis was forced to limp back to the pits, ultimately retiring from the race due to the damage. Nico continued but finished second, facing boos from the crowd during the podium ceremony.

The incident ignited a firestorm within the team and the broader Formula 1 community. Lewis was adamant that Nico had caused the collision deliberately or at least recklessly. In a heated post-race meeting, tensions erupted. Reports surfaced that Nico had admitted to making a point by not backing out of the move, though he denied any intention to cause a collision.

Team management responded swiftly. Mercedes' Executive Director Toto Wolff and Non-Executive Chairman Niki Lauda expressed their displeasure publicly. Wolff described the incident as "unacceptable," and Lauda lamented the loss of valuable points due to intra-team collisions. The team imposed internal sanctions and reiterated that such occurrences would not be tolerated.

The Belgian Grand Prix marked a turning point. Trust between Lewis and Nico eroded further, and the rivalry intensified. The incident underscored the challenges of managing two fiercely competitive drivers within the same team, each unwilling to yield in the pursuit of the championship.

Strain on Friendship

Media Portrayal of Tensions

The media played a significant role in amplifying the tensions between Lewis and Nico. Headlines and commentary often framed their rivalry in dramatic terms, highlighting conflicts and speculating on personal animosities. The narrative shifted from one of friendly competition to a more adversarial portrayal.

Journalists dissected every interaction, on and off the track, searching for signs of discord. Press conferences became arenas for probing questions, sometimes exacerbating the strains. Comments made in the heat of competition were scrutinized and, at times, sensationalized. The Monaco and Belgium incidents were particularly magnified, with pundits debating the drivers' intentions and character.

Social media added another layer of complexity. Fans took sides, often expressing vehement support or criticism of one driver over the other. The public discourse contributed to the pressure the drivers felt, knowing that their actions were under intense observation and subject to widespread interpretation.

Both drivers attempted to manage the media's influence. Lewis, wearing his emotions more openly, sometimes voiced his frustrations, which the media eagerly reported. Nico, typically more reserved, faced challenges in conveying his perspective without fueling further controversy. The team provided media training and guidance, but controlling the narrative proved difficult amidst the fervor.

Personal Interactions Off the Track

Off the track, the friendship between Lewis and Nico showed signs of strain. The trust and camaraderie that once defined their relationship were eroding under the weight of competition and the incidents that had unfolded. Their interactions became more formal and guarded, lacking the warmth of previous years.

Shared activities outside of racing diminished. Whereas they once might have spent leisure time together, they now focused on their individual routines and preparations. In team meetings and briefings, the atmosphere grew tense, with communication becoming more transactional.

Efforts by team management to facilitate reconciliation had limited success. Ross Brawn and Toto Wolff organized meetings to address issues and encourage open dialogue. While both drivers expressed a desire to maintain professionalism, the underlying tensions remained unresolved.

The personal rift was perhaps most poignantly illustrated at the Monaco Grand Prix. Following the qualifying controversy, Lewis and Nico reportedly did not speak, even as they shared the front row of the grid. The silence between them was a stark contrast to the friendly exchanges of the past.

Family members and close associates also felt the impact. Anthony Hamilton, Lewis's father, and Keke Rosberg, Nico's father, both former racers themselves, observed the changing dynamics with concern. They understood the pressures their sons faced but recognized that the rivalry was taking a personal toll.

Despite the strain, both drivers maintained a level of respect on a professional level. They continued to perform at the highest standard, pushing each other to excel. The competitive fire that drove them also served as a catalyst for their exceptional performances throughout the season.

The 2014 season was a crucible in which the rivalry between Lewis Hamilton and Nico Rosberg was forged and intensified. The combination of Mercedes' dominance and the new regulations created a unique environment where the two teammates were effectively in a league of their own. With the championship battle confined primarily between them, every race became a direct confrontation.

The incidents at Monaco and Belgium were pivotal moments that shifted the dynamics of their relationship. What had begun as a friendly competition evolved into a battle marked by mistrust and heightened emotions. The strain on their friendship was palpable, affecting not only their personal interactions but also the broader atmosphere within the team.

Mercedes faced the daunting task of managing this rivalry to prevent it from derailing their championship aspirations. Balancing the drivers' ambitions with team unity required careful strategy and sometimes difficult interventions. The team implemented clear guidelines and emphasized the importance of mutual respect and cooperation.

For Lewis and Nico, the season was a journey through uncharted territory. They grappled with the challenges of competing against a close friend under intense scrutiny and high stakes. The experiences of 2014 would leave lasting impressions on both men, shaping their approaches to competition and their perspectives on friendship and professionalism.

As the season drew to a close, the championship remained undecided, setting the stage for a dramatic conclusion. The events of 2014 had ignited a rivalry that would continue to burn brightly, influencing the narrative of Formula 1 in the years that followed. The interplay of technical excellence, personal ambition, and human emotion made for a compelling saga that resonated with fans and observers around the world.

Chapter 8: The 2015 Season—Tensions Rise

The 2015 Formula 1 season unfolded against a backdrop of heightened expectations and simmering tensions between Lewis Hamilton and Nico Rosberg. Mercedes continued to assert its dominance, and with a superior car at their disposal, the two teammates once again found themselves locked in a battle for the World Championship. The rivalry that ignited in the previous season intensified, permeating every aspect of their professional relationship. Psychological warfare, strategic maneuvering, and pivotal moments both on and off the track defined a year that tested the limits of their rivalry and the resilience of the Mercedes team.

Continued Dominance and Intensifying Rivalry

Close Championship Standings

Mercedes entered the 2015 season as the clear favorite, having secured both the Constructors' and Drivers' Championships the previous year. The W06 Hybrid, their new car, built upon the strengths of its predecessor. The engineering team refined the aerodynamics, improved the power unit's efficiency, and addressed reliability concerns. The result was a machine that once again outpaced its competitors by a considerable margin.

The season began with a strong statement from Mercedes at the Australian Grand Prix. Lewis Hamilton secured pole position and won the race comfortably, with Nico Rosberg finishing second. This one-two finish set the tone for the early part of the season. The two drivers alternated victories and podium finishes, keeping the championship standings tight.

By mid-season, Lewis had a slight lead, but Nico remained within striking distance.

Races like the Chinese Grand Prix and the Spanish Grand Prix showcased the team's dominance but also highlighted the growing friction between the drivers. In China, Nico accused Lewis of deliberately backing him into Sebastian Vettel's Ferrari during the race, compromising his strategy. Lewis dismissed the accusations, stating that his focus was on his own race and that he had done nothing untoward. The incident underscored the sensitivity between the teammates and foreshadowed further conflicts.

As the season progressed, the gap between Lewis and Nico fluctuated but remained close enough to keep the championship battle alive. Each driver was acutely aware that any mistake could swing the momentum. The pressure intensified with every race, amplifying the underlying tensions.

Psychological Warfare

Mind Games and Strategic Comments

The rivalry between Lewis and Nico extended beyond the confines of the racetrack. Psychological warfare became a prominent feature of their interactions, as each sought to gain an edge over the other. Mind games manifested in various forms, from subtle remarks in interviews to strategic positioning during practice sessions.

Lewis, known for his confidence and charisma, often spoke about his performances in ways that emphasized his strengths. He would highlight his ability to perform under pressure, his skill in wet conditions, or his superior racecraft.

While not overtly disparaging Nico, these comments served to reinforce his own status as the lead driver.

Nico, typically more reserved, began to adopt a more assertive stance. He challenged Lewis's narratives by emphasizing teamwork and questioning decisions that he felt disadvantaged him. For example, after the Monaco Grand Prix, where a strategic error by the team cost Lewis a likely victory, Nico expressed sympathy but also noted that luck played a role in racing.

The use of social media added another dimension to the psychological battle. Posts and messages that seemed innocuous to the public carried deeper meanings for those within the team. A well-timed photo or a cryptic comment could be interpreted as a jab or a show of confidence. Both drivers were mindful of their public images but also leveraged these platforms to project strength.

Press Conference Confrontations

Press conferences became arenas for verbal sparring. Journalists, eager to uncover stories, often probed the drivers with pointed questions about their relationship and on-track incidents. The responses provided insights into their mindsets and occasionally escalated tensions.

One notable exchange occurred during the build-up to the Japanese Grand Prix. A reporter asked about the dynamics within the team and whether the rivalry was affecting performance. Lewis responded by emphasizing his focus on winning and dismissed any suggestions of discord. Nico, when asked the same question, remarked that while competition was natural, certain actions both on and off the track had strained their relationship.

In another instance, following the United States Grand Prix, the drivers were asked about the cap-throwing incident (which will be detailed later). The tension was palpable as they sat side by side, each carefully choosing their words. Lewis downplayed the significance, suggesting it was a minor disagreement, while Nico expressed frustration over the situation.

These confrontations were not only between the drivers but also involved team management. Toto Wolff and Niki Lauda occasionally stepped in during press conferences to defuse situations or provide diplomatic answers. The media's focus on the rivalry added pressure on the team to present a united front, even as internal conflicts simmered.

Significant Events

U.S. Grand Prix Cap-Throwing Incident

One of the most symbolic moments of the 2015 season occurred at the United States Grand Prix in Austin, Texas. Lewis Hamilton entered the race with the opportunity to clinch his third World Championship title. The race was filled with drama, including challenging weather conditions and multiple lead changes between the Mercedes drivers.

In the closing stages, Nico Rosberg led the race but made a crucial mistake, running wide at Turn 12 due to a gust of wind causing a wheelspin. Lewis seized the opportunity and overtook Nico to take the lead. Despite Nico's efforts to regain the position, Lewis held on to win the race and secure the championship.

After the race, the atmosphere was tense. In the cool-down room, where drivers gather before the podium ceremony, an incident unfolded that encapsulated the strained relationship between the teammates. As they waited, Lewis picked up a Pirelli-branded baseball cap labeled "2nd" and tossed it towards Nico. The gesture was perceived as either a casual act or a subtle taunt. Nico, visibly displeased, threw the cap back towards Lewis in a dismissive manner.

The moment was caught on camera and quickly circulated in the media. It became a symbol of the deteriorating relationship between the drivers. Some interpreted Lewis's action as insensitive, given the emotional context, while others viewed Nico's reaction as a sign of poor sportsmanship.

In the subsequent press conference, Nico expressed his frustration, citing the race incident where he felt Lewis had been too aggressive at the start, pushing him wide at the first corner. Lewis defended his actions, stating that it was a fair racing move and that winning the championship was his primary focus.

The cap-throwing incident highlighted the personal tensions that had been building throughout the season. It was a tangible expression of the underlying resentment and competitiveness that had overshadowed their once-friendly relationship.

Team Orders and Their Impacts

Team orders became a contentious issue during the 2015 season. Mercedes, keen to maximize their results and manage the rivalry, occasionally issued directives to the drivers to maintain positions or adopt specific strategies. These orders were met with varying degrees of compliance and often fueled further discord.

At the Chinese Grand Prix, as mentioned earlier, Nico accused Lewis of deliberately slowing down to compromise his race. The team had instructed both drivers to manage their pace to preserve tires, but the interpretation of these instructions became a point of contention. Nico felt disadvantaged, believing that Lewis's actions were detrimental to the team's overall performance.

In Austria, team orders were again a topic of debate. The drivers were advised to avoid unnecessary risks when racing each other. Despite this, they engaged in close battles, prompting concerns from the pit wall. The team reminded them of the importance of securing maximum points without jeopardizing the result through collisions or aggressive maneuvers.

The most significant instance occurred at the Japanese Grand Prix. With Lewis leading the race and Nico in second, the team requested that both drivers hold position to ensure a one-two finish. Nico, eager to challenge for the win, was frustrated by the directive but ultimately complied. The decision reignited discussions about the balance between individual ambition and team strategy.

These incidents had a cumulative effect on the drivers' attitudes toward the team and each other. Lewis felt justified in pursuing victories without undue restrictions, while Nico perceived a bias in the team's handling of situations. The lack of trust extended beyond their personal relationship to include the broader team dynamics.

Toto Wolff and Niki Lauda faced the complex task of managing these issues. They held meetings with the drivers to address concerns, emphasizing the importance of team unity and adherence to agreed-upon guidelines. However, the effectiveness of these interventions was limited, as the underlying competitive tensions persisted.

Conclusion of the Season

As the 2015 season drew to a close, Lewis Hamilton secured his third World Championship title with three races remaining. His performance throughout the year was marked by consistency, speed, and strategic acumen. Nico Rosberg, despite strong showings and multiple victories, was left to reflect on missed opportunities and the widening gap between himself and his teammate.

In the final races, Nico rallied to win in Mexico, Brazil, and Abu Dhabi, securing second place in the championship and ending the season on a positive note. These victories provided a psychological boost and set the stage for renewed determination in the following year.

The tensions that characterized the season had lasting implications. The relationship between Lewis and Nico had evolved from friendship to rivalry and now bordered on antagonism. The psychological warfare, public confrontations, and significant events like the cap-throwing incident had eroded the trust and camaraderie they once shared.

Mercedes faced the ongoing challenge of managing this dynamic while maintaining their competitive edge. The team recognized that the rivalry, while pushing both drivers to excel, also posed risks to team harmony and performance. Strategies for the upcoming season would need to address these complexities.

The 2015 season was a pivotal chapter in the saga of Lewis Hamilton and Nico Rosberg. It was a year where tensions rose to new heights, fueled by close championship standings, psychological battles, and significant events that tested their professional and personal boundaries. The rivalry intensified, moving beyond the confines of sport into a realm where emotions ran deep and consequences extended beyond the racetrack.

For Lewis, the season solidified his status as one of the sport's elite drivers. His ability to perform under pressure and navigate the complexities of competition affirmed his championship credentials. For Nico, the challenges of the year prompted introspection and a renewed commitment to overcoming obstacles.

The stage was set for the next phase of their rivalry. With the 2016 season looming, both drivers prepared for what would become one of the most intense and consequential battles in Formula 1 history. The lessons learned, the wounds inflicted, and the determination forged in 2015 would all play a role in shaping the events to come.

Chapter 9: The 2016 Season—The Final Showdown

The 2016 Formula 1 season stands as one of the most dramatic and emotionally charged chapters in the saga of Lewis Hamilton and Nico Rosberg. After years of rivalry, tension, and intense competition, the two Mercedes teammates entered the season with the stakes higher than ever. For Rosberg, it was a quest to step out of Hamilton's shadow and claim his first World Championship. For Hamilton, it was an opportunity to assert his dominance and secure a fourth title. The season unfolded with a series of twists, turns, and climactic moments that culminated in a showdown for the ages.

Rosberg's Strong Start

Winning the First Four Races

Nico Rosberg began the 2016 season with remarkable momentum. Building on his victories in the final three races of the previous year, he extended his winning streak to seven consecutive Grands Prix by triumphing in the first four races of the new season. His performances were a statement of intent, signaling that he was a formidable contender for the championship.

- **Australian Grand Prix**: Rosberg capitalized on a strategic pit stop and tire management to overtake early leader Sebastian Vettel and secure victory. Hamilton, after a poor start that dropped him to sixth, recovered to finish second, but the result gave Rosberg an early lead in the standings.

- **Bahrain Grand Prix**: A strong start from pole position allowed Rosberg to control the race, while Hamilton was involved in a first-corner collision with Valtteri Bottas, damaging his car and compromising his race. Despite this, Hamilton fought back to finish third, but Rosberg's lead widened.

- **Chinese Grand Prix**: Rosberg dominated the race, while Hamilton started from the back due to a power unit failure in qualifying. Hamilton's struggles continued with damage from early contact, and he finished seventh. Rosberg's victory extended his championship lead significantly.

- **Russian Grand Prix**: Rosberg secured a grand slam by taking pole position, fastest lap, and leading every lap of the race. Hamilton, hindered by mechanical issues in qualifying, started from tenth but skillfully navigated through the field to finish second. Nonetheless, Rosberg's flawless performance reinforced his advantage.

Rosberg's strong start was fueled by a combination of excellent driving, reliability, and strategic acumen. He appeared more focused and determined than ever, exhibiting confidence that he could finally dethrone Hamilton. The early successes bolstered his morale and placed psychological pressure on his teammate.

Hamilton's Fightback

Mid-Season Resurgence

Facing a substantial points deficit, Lewis Hamilton needed to respond decisively to keep his championship hopes alive.

Demonstrating resilience and tenacity, he mounted a mid-season resurgence that reignited the title battle.

- **Spanish Grand Prix**: The race ended disastrously for both Mercedes drivers (detailed later), but Hamilton regrouped for the subsequent rounds.

- **Monaco Grand Prix**: In challenging wet conditions, Hamilton delivered a masterful performance. Capitalizing on strategic errors by rival teams and showcasing his skill in slippery conditions, he secured his first victory of the season. Rosberg, struggling with brake temperatures, finished seventh.

- **Canadian Grand Prix**: Hamilton won again, executing a strategic one-stop race and fending off Sebastian Vettel's Ferrari. Rosberg faced setbacks, including a first-corner clash with Hamilton and a late spin, finishing fifth.

- **Austrian Grand Prix**: The race featured a dramatic last-lap collision between the Mercedes drivers (detailed later), but Hamilton emerged victorious, closing the points gap.

- **British Grand Prix**: Hamilton dominated his home race at Silverstone, leading from start to finish. Rosberg finished second but received a time penalty for breaching radio communication rules, demoting him to third.

Hamilton's series of victories and consistent podium finishes eroded Rosberg's early lead. By the Hungarian Grand Prix, Hamilton had overtaken Rosberg in the championship standings. His fightback was characterized by exceptional driving under pressure, strategic insight, and a refusal to concede defeat.

Climactic Moments

Spanish Grand Prix Collision Eliminating Both Cars

The Spanish Grand Prix at the Circuit de Barcelona-Catalunya became a defining moment in the 2016 season. Starting from the front row, Rosberg overtook Hamilton at the first corner, seizing the lead. As they exited Turn 3, Hamilton, perceiving an opportunity, attempted to overtake Rosberg on the inside. Rosberg moved to defend his position, forcing Hamilton onto the grass. Losing control, Hamilton spun and collided with Rosberg, resulting in both cars crashing out of the race.

The incident was a catastrophic outcome for Mercedes, marking the first time since their return as a works team that both cars were eliminated on the first lap. Team management, including Toto Wolff and Niki Lauda, were visibly frustrated and summoned the drivers for immediate discussions.

An investigation by the stewards ruled it a racing incident, attributing no specific blame to either driver. However, internally, tensions escalated. Hamilton felt that Rosberg had been overly aggressive in defending, while Rosberg maintained that he had the right to protect his position.

The crash intensified the rivalry and underscored the risks inherent in their fierce competition. Mercedes implemented new guidelines, warning both drivers that such incidents were unacceptable and could lead to disciplinary actions, including potential race suspensions.

Austrian Grand Prix Last-Lap Crash

The Austrian Grand Prix at the Red Bull Ring presented another dramatic confrontation between Hamilton and Rosberg. Starting from pole, Hamilton led initially but lost the lead to Rosberg during the pit stop phase. As the race unfolded, Hamilton closed the gap, setting the stage for a final-lap showdown.

On the last lap, Hamilton attempted an overtake on the outside heading into Turn 2. Rosberg, defending the inside line, failed to turn in adequately, resulting in contact between the two cars. Hamilton was forced wide but managed to continue and win the race. Rosberg sustained front wing damage and fell to fourth place by the finish.

The collision sparked immediate controversy. Hamilton criticized Rosberg's defensive tactics, suggesting they were overly aggressive and unsportsmanlike. Rosberg blamed brake issues and maintained that he had the right to defend his position.

Mercedes launched an investigation, revealing that Rosberg had suffered brake-by-wire failure, but also noted that he had not left sufficient space as per racing regulations. The team reprimanded Rosberg and emphasized that such incidents jeopardized their objectives.

The Austrian Grand Prix incident further strained the relationship between the drivers and challenged the team's ability to manage their rivalry. The stakes were higher than ever, and the margin for error had evaporated.

Championship Decider

Abu Dhabi Grand Prix Tension

Entering the final race of the season at the Yas Marina Circuit in Abu Dhabi, Nico Rosberg led the championship by 12 points. The title scenario was clear: if Rosberg finished on the podium, he would secure his first World Championship, regardless of Hamilton's result. For Hamilton, winning the race was essential, but he also needed Rosberg to finish fourth or lower.

Qualifying saw Hamilton take pole position, with Rosberg alongside him on the front row. The tension was palpable, with immense pressure on both drivers. The team reiterated the importance of a clean race and adherence to team protocols.

At the start, Hamilton maintained the lead, with Rosberg settling into second. Throughout the race, Hamilton controlled the pace, but an underlying strategy emerged. Aware that merely winning was insufficient, Hamilton began to back Rosberg into the pursuing cars of Sebastian Vettel and Max Verstappen, hoping they would overtake Rosberg and push him off the podium.

Mercedes issued several radio messages to Hamilton, instructing him to increase his pace. Hamilton questioned these directives, stating, "I'm losing the World Championship, so right now, I'm not bothered if I win or lose this race." The team's requests became more urgent, but Hamilton persisted in his tactic.

The situation created a dramatic finale. Vettel closed in on Rosberg, pressuring him in the closing laps. Rosberg remained composed, defending his position skillfully. Despite the challenges, he crossed the line in second place behind Hamilton, securing the World Championship by five points.

Rosberg Clinches the Title

Nico Rosberg's championship victory was the culmination of years of dedication, perseverance, and overcoming adversity. He became the second son of a World Champion to win the title himself, following in the footsteps of his father, Keke Rosberg, the 1982 champion.

The achievement was a personal triumph, validating his efforts to emerge from Hamilton's shadow and affirming his place among the elite drivers of his generation. Rosberg's consistency, strategic acumen, and ability to withstand immense pressure were key factors in his success.

For Hamilton, the result was a bitter disappointment. Despite winning the race and demonstrating exceptional skill throughout the season, he fell short of securing the title. Mechanical failures earlier in the year, including engine issues in Malaysia where he retired from the lead, had undermined his campaign.

The Abu Dhabi Grand Prix encapsulated the complexities of their rivalry. Hamilton's tactics, while within the rules, raised ethical questions and tested team unity. Rosberg's resilience under pressure showcased his growth as a driver and competitor.

Aftermath

Emotions and Reactions from Both Drivers

In the immediate aftermath of the race, emotions ran high. On the podium, Rosberg was jubilant, celebrating with genuine joy and relief. Hamilton offered a subdued congratulation but appeared visibly disappointed. The dynamics between them were tense, reflecting the intensity of their rivalry.

During the post-race interviews, Rosberg expressed gratitude to his team, family, and supporters. He acknowledged the challenges and praised Hamilton as a formidable competitor. The victory, he said, was the fulfillment of a lifelong dream.

Hamilton congratulated Rosberg but also alluded to the difficulties he faced during the season. He mentioned the mechanical issues and suggested that luck had not been on his side. When asked about his tactics during the race, he defended his approach, stating that he did everything within the rules to try to win the championship.

The media dissected the events, with opinions divided on Hamilton's actions and the broader implications for their relationship. Some criticized Hamilton for defying team orders, while others argued that his actions were understandable given the stakes.

Rosberg's Retirement Announcement

In a stunning development five days after winning the championship, Nico Rosberg announced his retirement from Formula 1. The decision shocked the motorsport world, including his team and rival. Rosberg cited the immense effort required to achieve his goal and a desire to focus on his family as reasons for stepping away.

He stated, "I have climbed my mountain, I am on the peak, so this feels right." Rosberg's retirement was a rare move for a reigning World Champion and sparked widespread discussion about the pressures of the sport.

Hamilton reacted with surprise, acknowledging that he had not anticipated Rosberg's decision. He expressed respect for Rosberg's choice and wished him well. However, the departure left a void in their rivalry and raised questions about the future dynamics within Mercedes.

Reflections and Legacy

The 2016 season marked the end of an era in the Hamilton-Rosberg rivalry. Their battles had pushed both drivers to new heights, but the toll on their friendship and personal lives was significant. Rosberg's retirement closed a chapter that had defined much of their careers.

For Hamilton, the loss of his primary competitor within the team presented new challenges. Mercedes would need to find a suitable replacement, and Hamilton would need to adapt to a new teammate dynamic.

The legacy of their rivalry is complex. It showcased the pinnacle of competitive spirit, driving technological advancements and captivating audiences worldwide. It also highlighted the strains that such intense competition can place on relationships, ethics, and personal well-being.

The 2016 season was the final showdown between Lewis Hamilton and Nico Rosberg—a culmination of years of rivalry, friendship, and professional competition. It was a season that tested their limits, both on and off the track, and delivered some of the most memorable moments in Formula 1 history.

Rosberg's strong start, Hamilton's determined fightback, and the climactic incidents that punctuated the season created a narrative rich with drama and emotion. The championship decider in Abu Dhabi encapsulated the essence of their rivalry, with both drivers exhibiting exceptional skill and unwavering determination.

The aftermath of the season brought closure to their storied relationship. Rosberg's retirement was a surprising and poignant conclusion, reflecting the personal costs of pursuing greatness. Hamilton, ever the competitor, faced new horizons and the opportunity to forge a different path.

The final showdown between Hamilton and Rosberg left an indelible mark on the sport. Their rivalry elevated the standards of competition, challenged notions of teamwork and individual ambition, and provided a compelling human story within the high-speed world of Formula 1.

As the dust settled, the lessons and memories of their battles remained—a testament to the complexities of pursuing excellence in a field where the margins between victory and defeat are razor-thin. The 2016 season stands as a defining chapter in their careers and a pivotal moment in the annals of motorsport.

Chapter 10: Behind the Scenes—Team Dynamics and Politics

The rivalry between Lewis Hamilton and Nico Rosberg was not confined to the racetrack; it permeated every facet of the Mercedes AMG Petronas Formula One Team. Behind the scenes, team management and staff navigated a complex landscape of competition, collaboration, and interpersonal dynamics. Central to this effort were Toto Wolff and Niki Lauda, whose leadership aimed to harness the strengths of both drivers while maintaining team cohesion. The challenges of managing two world-class talents extended to the technical teams and support staff, where perceptions of favoritism and internal politics tested the resilience and unity of the organization.

Mercedes Management Strategies

Toto Wolff and Niki Lauda's Roles

Toto Wolff and Niki Lauda were instrumental in shaping the Mercedes team's approach to the Hamilton-Rosberg rivalry. Their leadership combined strategic vision, racing expertise, and an understanding of the human elements that influence performance.

Toto Wolff, as the Executive Director and later Team Principal, was responsible for the overall management of the team. A former racing driver and successful investor, Wolff brought a business acumen and a focus on cultivating a high-performance culture. He emphasized transparency, accountability, and continuous improvement. Wolff recognized that managing the dynamics between Hamilton and Rosberg required balancing individual ambitions with collective goals.

Niki Lauda, a three-time Formula 1 World Champion, served as the Non-Executive Chairman. His experience as a driver who had navigated intense rivalries provided valuable insights. Lauda acted as a mentor and mediator, offering guidance based on his own storied career. His direct communication style and reputation commanded respect from both drivers.

Together, Wolff and Lauda formed a leadership duo that complemented each other's strengths. They were united in their commitment to ensuring Mercedes remained at the pinnacle of the sport while navigating the complexities of having two top-tier drivers in direct competition.

Efforts to Manage the Rivalry

Managing the rivalry between Hamilton and Rosberg required proactive strategies and interventions. Wolff and Lauda implemented several measures to mitigate conflicts and foster a productive environment.

Establishing Clear Team Policies: Early in the rivalry, the management outlined explicit guidelines for on-track behavior. After incidents like the collision at the 2014 Belgian Grand Prix, Wolff and Lauda convened meetings to reinforce the expectations. The drivers were reminded of the team's priorities and the consequences of jeopardizing results through unnecessary risks.

Open Communication Channels: Regular debriefings and meetings were organized to facilitate open dialogue. The leadership encouraged both drivers to voice concerns and discuss issues directly. By creating forums for candid conversations, Wolff and Lauda aimed to prevent misunderstandings and address tensions before they escalated.

Equal Treatment Commitment: To prevent perceptions of bias, the team emphasized equal treatment in terms of equipment, resources, and opportunities. Both drivers had access to the same technical data and support. Wolff often reiterated that the team did not favor one driver over the other, aiming to maintain fairness and integrity.

Intervention in Conflicts: When incidents occurred, such as the 2016 Spanish Grand Prix collision, Wolff and Lauda acted swiftly. They held individual and joint meetings with the drivers to dissect the events and reinforce the importance of team objectives. Penalties and warnings were issued when necessary, signaling that actions detrimental to the team would not be tolerated.

Psychological Support: Recognizing the mental strain of the rivalry, the team provided access to sports psychologists and support staff. The goal was to help the drivers manage stress, maintain focus, and develop coping strategies. This support extended to other team members affected by the high-pressure environment.

Promoting Team Unity: Team-building activities and events were organized to strengthen relationships among all personnel. By fostering a sense of camaraderie and shared purpose, Wolff and Lauda sought to mitigate divisions that could arise from the drivers' rivalry.

Media Management: The leadership was mindful of the media's role in amplifying tensions. They provided media training for the drivers and staff, encouraging consistent messaging that emphasized team unity. Wolff and Lauda also engaged with the media strategically to control narratives and reduce speculation.

Despite these efforts, the intensity of the rivalry presented ongoing challenges. Wolff acknowledged in interviews that managing two competitive drivers was "like having two alpha males in the team," requiring constant vigilance and adaptability. Lauda, drawing on his experience, sometimes took a more personal approach, engaging in one-on-one conversations to appeal to the drivers' professionalism and shared history.

Technical Teams and Support Staff

Allegations of Favoritism

Within the high-stakes environment of Formula 1, perceptions of favoritism can emerge, especially when two drivers are in direct competition. At Mercedes, rumors and allegations occasionally surfaced, suggesting that certain engineers or mechanics favored one driver over the other.

Structural Organization: The team operated with two separate car crews, each dedicated to one driver. While this structure is standard in Formula 1, it can inadvertently create silos and foster loyalty to a specific driver. The close working relationships between drivers and their respective engineers and mechanics can intensify these dynamics.

Engineer Assignments: In 2016, there were reports that some key technical personnel shifted between the drivers' crews. For instance, Hamilton's long-time performance engineer, Jock Clear, left the team to join Ferrari. Such changes fueled speculation about internal politics and potential impacts on performance.

Communication of Technical Data: Mercedes maintained a policy of sharing all technical data between both sides of the garage. However, there were instances where one driver expressed concerns about the timing or completeness of information sharing. Any delays or discrepancies were scrutinized and sometimes interpreted as signs of favoritism.

Drivers' Comments: Both Hamilton and Rosberg, at different times, hinted at perceived inequalities. Hamilton occasionally expressed frustrations over strategic decisions or reliability issues, suggesting that luck or other factors were not evenly distributed. Rosberg also alluded to moments where he felt disadvantaged.

It's important to note that no concrete evidence substantiated allegations of systemic favoritism within Mercedes. Team management consistently denied any bias, emphasizing their commitment to fairness. Toto Wolff stated, "We have no number one driver; both have equal status and equal opportunities."

Impact on Team Morale

The rivalry and associated tensions had a ripple effect on team morale. The technical teams and support staff found themselves navigating a delicate balance between supporting their assigned driver and contributing to the collective success of Mercedes.

Stress and Pressure: The relentless pursuit of excellence, combined with the drivers' competition, created a high-pressure environment. Team members faced long hours, tight deadlines, and the emotional toll of the rivalry. Maintaining peak performance under such conditions was challenging.

Internal Divisions: While the team strove for unity, subtle divisions occasionally emerged. Crew members might feel a stronger allegiance to their driver, especially during moments of conflict. This could lead to strained interactions between different groups within the team.

Motivation and Engagement: Success on the track often boosted morale, but setbacks or internal conflicts had the opposite effect. The double retirement in Spain (2016) and collisions between the drivers were demoralizing events. Team members invested significant effort into preparing the cars, and such incidents felt like squandered opportunities.

Management's Role in Mitigation: Wolff and Lauda recognized the importance of addressing morale issues proactively. They increased communication with staff, provided reassurances, and acknowledged the team's hard work. Efforts were made to celebrate collective achievements and reinforce the value of every team member's contribution.

Cultural Initiatives: Mercedes implemented programs to promote well-being and teamwork. This included providing resources for stress management, organizing social events, and encouraging feedback from all levels of the organization. The aim was to foster an inclusive culture where individuals felt valued beyond the drivers' rivalry.

Impact on Performance: Despite the challenges, the team's performance remained exceptional. Mercedes continued to dominate the Constructors' Championship, a testament to the professionalism and dedication of the staff. The ability to compartmentalize the drivers' rivalry and focus on common goals was a strength of the organization.

Lessons Learned: The experiences during this period prompted reflections on leadership and team dynamics. Mercedes recognized that managing human factors was as crucial as technical excellence. The insights gained influenced future approaches to team management, including strategies for integrating new drivers and maintaining harmony.

The behind-the-scenes dynamics at Mercedes during the Hamilton-Rosberg era reveal a complex interplay of competition, collaboration, and human psychology. The leadership of Toto Wolff and Niki Lauda was pivotal in navigating these challenges. Their efforts to manage the rivalry, uphold fairness, and maintain team morale were integral to the team's sustained success.

The allegations of favoritism and the impact on support staff underscore the delicate balance required in high-performance teams. Perceptions, even if unfounded, can influence attitudes and behaviors. Addressing these issues transparently and fostering a culture of trust are essential.

The Mercedes team's experience highlights broader themes relevant to any competitive organization. The pursuit of individual excellence must be aligned with collective objectives. Effective leadership involves not only strategic decision-making but also empathy, communication, and the ability to unify diverse talents toward a shared vision.

The Hamilton-Rosberg rivalry, while presenting significant challenges, also drove the team to new heights. The intensity pushed technological innovations, strategic advancements, and personal growth for those involved. The lessons learned during this period continue to inform Mercedes' approach and contribute to their ongoing success in Formula 1.

As the chapter closes on this era, the behind-the-scenes stories add depth to the public narrative. They illuminate the complexities of managing elite athletes in a team context and the intricate dynamics that define success at the highest levels of motorsport. The legacy of this period is a testament to the resilience and adaptability of both individuals and the organization as a whole.

Chapter 11: The Psychological Battle

The rivalry between Lewis Hamilton and Nico Rosberg was not just a contest of speed and skill on the racetrack; it was also a profound psychological duel. As teammates competing for the highest honors in Formula 1, they were locked in a mental struggle that tested their resilience, strategic thinking, and emotional fortitude. The pressures of elite competition, amplified by intense media scrutiny and personal expectations, created a landscape where mental strengths and weaknesses could make the difference between victory and defeat. This chapter delves into how each driver coped under pressure, the role of the media in fueling their rivalry, and the personal sacrifices they made in pursuit of greatness.

Mental Strengths and Weaknesses

How Each Driver Coped Under Pressure

Lewis Hamilton possessed a natural confidence and charisma that often translated into psychological advantages on the track. His ability to perform under pressure was evident from his earliest days in Formula 1. Hamilton thrived in high-stakes situations, displaying remarkable composure during crucial moments. His instinctive driving style was complemented by a mental toughness that allowed him to recover quickly from setbacks.

Hamilton's upbringing played a significant role in shaping his mental resilience. Facing challenges and overcoming obstacles from a young age instilled in him a determination to succeed against the odds. He often spoke about channeling negativity into motivation, using doubts and criticisms as fuel to push himself further. This mindset enabled him to handle the pressures of being a high-profile athlete and the expectations that came with his success.

However, Hamilton was not immune to the strains of competition. There were times when emotions surfaced, revealing vulnerabilities. Instances of frustration with team decisions, mechanical failures, or on-track incidents sometimes led to candid expressions of dissatisfaction. Yet, he generally managed to refocus and regain his composure, turning adversity into an impetus for improvement.

Nico Rosberg, on the other hand, was known for his analytical approach and meticulous preparation. He relied on a strong work ethic, attention to detail, and a strategic mindset to gain advantages. Rosberg invested significant time in understanding technical aspects, studying data, and refining his performance. His mental strength was characterized by discipline and perseverance.

Rosberg faced the challenge of competing against a teammate who had a more naturally aggressive and instinctive style. To cope, he sought to optimize every element within his control. He worked closely with engineers, focused on fitness, and employed psychological techniques to enhance concentration and resilience.

Under pressure, Rosberg sometimes exhibited signs of tension. The intense rivalry with Hamilton, coupled with the high expectations placed upon him, created moments of stress. Notably, after critical incidents or defeats, he appeared visibly affected. However, Rosberg also demonstrated the capacity to learn from setbacks. His ability to bounce back, particularly in the 2016 season, showcased his mental fortitude.

Interplay Between Their Mentalities

The contrasting mental approaches of Hamilton and Rosberg added layers to their rivalry. Hamilton's confidence could be both a source of intimidation and irritation for Rosberg. Conversely, Rosberg's methodical strategies sometimes unsettled Hamilton, who preferred a more spontaneous approach.

Their psychological battle extended to qualifying sessions, race starts, and strategic decisions during races. Each driver sought to outwit the other, not just in terms of raw speed but also through mind games and tactical ploys. The mental duel was as significant as the physical one, influencing their performances and the outcomes of races.

Key Moments Highlighting Mental Dynamics

- **Monaco Grand Prix 2014**: The qualifying controversy, where Rosberg's off-track excursion prevented Hamilton from potentially taking pole position, had psychological ramifications. Hamilton's suspicions about Rosberg's intentions added strain, affecting their trust.

- **United States Grand Prix 2015**: The cap-throwing incident after Hamilton clinched the championship was emblematic of the psychological tensions. Rosberg's frustration was palpable, reflecting the emotional toll of their rivalry.

- **Abu Dhabi Grand Prix 2016**: Hamilton's deliberate slowing of pace to back Rosberg into other competitors was a strategic move that tested Rosberg's composure. Rosberg's ability to maintain focus and secure the necessary position demonstrated mental resilience.

Media Influence

Role of Journalists in Fueling the Rivalry

The media played a significant role in shaping and amplifying the Hamilton-Rosberg rivalry. Journalists, commentators, and pundits scrutinized every aspect of their relationship, often highlighting conflicts and speculating on underlying tensions. The constant spotlight intensified the psychological pressure on both drivers.

Sensationalism and Narrative Building

Media outlets frequently portrayed the rivalry as a dramatic narrative, emphasizing personal conflicts and dramatic incidents. Headlines and stories were crafted to capture attention, sometimes oversimplifying complex situations or exaggerating disputes. This sensationalism contributed to a public perception of animosity, even when the reality was more nuanced.

Provocative Questioning

During press conferences and interviews, journalists often posed provocative questions designed to elicit revealing or controversial responses. Queries about trust, teamwork, and past incidents forced the drivers to address sensitive topics publicly. The pressure to respond appropriately added to their mental burden.

For example, after the Belgian Grand Prix collision in 2014, both drivers faced intense media scrutiny. Questions about blame and intent were persistent, requiring careful navigation to avoid inflaming the situation further.

Social Media Amplification

The rise of social media amplified the media's influence. Fans and commentators shared articles, videos, and opinions widely, creating a constant stream of content related to the rivalry. Misinterpretations or out-of-context quotes could spread rapidly, impacting public perception and adding pressure on the drivers to manage their images.

Impact on Team Dynamics

The media's focus on internal team matters sometimes strained Mercedes' efforts to manage the rivalry. Leaked information, speculative reports, and public debates about team orders or favoritism complicated the leadership's strategies. The drivers had to contend not only with their personal competition but also with external narratives that could affect morale and unity.

Drivers' Responses to Media Pressure

Both Hamilton and Rosberg developed strategies to cope with media influence. Hamilton often used media opportunities to convey confidence and reinforce his mindset. He engaged with fans through social media, sharing insights into his life and perspectives.

Rosberg tended to be more guarded, carefully considering his words to avoid misinterpretation. He occasionally expressed frustration with media intrusion but recognized the importance of maintaining professionalism.

Media as a Psychological Tool

At times, the drivers utilized the media to their advantage. Strategic comments or subtle remarks could serve as mind games, attempting to unsettle the opponent or gain a psychological edge. This interplay added another dimension to their rivalry, where public statements became part of the competition.

Personal Sacrifices

The Toll on Personal Lives and Relationships

The relentless pursuit of success in Formula 1 demanded significant personal sacrifices from both Lewis Hamilton and Nico Rosberg. The intensity of their rivalry, combined with the pressures of the sport, impacted their personal lives and relationships in profound ways.

Strain on Friendship

Hamilton and Rosberg's friendship, dating back to their karting days, was tested to its limits. The competition for championships eroded trust and camaraderie. Moments of conflict and suspicion replaced earlier times of shared experiences and mutual support.

The deterioration of their relationship was a personal loss for both. The joy of competing alongside a friend transformed into the stress of confronting a rival. Attempts to reconcile or maintain friendship were often overshadowed by the demands of their professional roles.

Family Considerations

For Rosberg, family played a crucial role in his life and career decisions. The pressures of competing at the highest level affected his personal time and relationships. After winning the World Championship in 2016, he cited the desire to spend more time with his wife and young daughter as a key factor in his decision to retire. The sacrifices required to maintain his competitive edge were no longer aligned with his personal priorities.

Hamilton's commitment to his career also influenced his personal life. Balancing a demanding schedule with relationships and personal interests was a constant challenge. He often spoke about the isolation that can come with success and the need to make difficult choices to remain at the top of his game.

Emotional and Physical Well-being

The mental and emotional toll of the rivalry manifested in stress, fatigue, and moments of doubt. Both drivers had to manage the psychological impact of defeats, criticism, and the relentless expectations placed upon them.

Sleep, nutrition, and physical health were meticulously managed, but the cumulative effects of pressure could not always be mitigated. The need for constant vigilance and the fear of losing ground to the rival added layers of stress that extended beyond the racetrack.

Social Life and Personal Interests

Personal hobbies and social activities were often curtailed to focus on training, preparation, and recovery. The demands of the sport left little time for leisure or relaxation. Travel schedules, media obligations, and team commitments dominated their calendars.

Hamilton, known for his interests in music, fashion, and philanthropy, sought to integrate these pursuits into his life. However, balancing them with his racing career required careful planning and sometimes led to criticisms about his focus.

Rosberg, valuing privacy and family time, often withdrew from public engagements to recharge. The need to maintain peak performance meant prioritizing professional responsibilities over personal desires.

Legacy and Reflection

The sacrifices made by both drivers were part of their dedication to excellence. However, they also prompted reflections on what was truly important. Rosberg's retirement decision was a clear acknowledgment of the personal costs associated with his ambitions.

For Hamilton, the journey continued, but not without recognition of the challenges. He has spoken about the importance of mental health, support networks, and finding balance in life.

Impact on Future Relationships

The experiences during their rivalry influenced how both drivers approached relationships within and outside the sport. Trust became a more guarded commodity, and lessons learned shaped interactions with new teammates, colleagues, and even family members.

The psychological battle between Lewis Hamilton and Nico Rosberg was a defining aspect of their rivalry. It extended beyond physical competition into realms of mental strength, media manipulation, and personal sacrifice. Their contrasting approaches to pressure, the influence of external narratives, and the costs incurred in their personal lives added depth to their story.

Understanding the psychological dimensions provides insight into the human side of high-performance sport. The demands placed on elite athletes are immense, and the mental challenges are as significant as the physical ones. The Hamilton-Rosberg rivalry serves as a case study in how psychological factors can influence outcomes, relationships, and individual well-being.

Their journey underscores the importance of mental resilience, effective coping strategies, and the recognition of personal limits. It also highlights the role of media and public perception in shaping the experiences of athletes. The sacrifices they made were profound, reflecting the complexities of pursuing greatness in a fiercely competitive environment.

As their careers evolved, both drivers adapted and grew, carrying forward the lessons learned from their psychological battles. Their experiences contributed to broader conversations about mental health, athlete support, and the balance between professional ambition and personal fulfillment.

The psychological battle was an integral part of the Hamilton-Rosberg rivalry, adding layers of intrigue and humanity to a story that captivated the world of motorsport. It reminds us that behind the helmets and high-speed action are individuals navigating the challenges of competition, identity, and the pursuit of dreams.

Chapter 12: Rosberg's Retirement—An Unexpected Farewell

The 2016 Formula 1 season culminated in a dramatic climax as Nico Rosberg clinched his first World Championship title. Just days later, the motorsport world was left stunned by an announcement that no one saw coming: Rosberg declared his retirement from Formula 1 with immediate effect. The decision sent shockwaves through the F1 community, sparking a flurry of reactions and raising questions about the reasons behind such an unexpected farewell. This chapter delves into the timing and motivations of Rosberg's retirement, the myriad responses from fans and colleagues, Lewis Hamilton's personal and public reactions, and the lasting impact of Rosberg's decision on his legacy.

Announcement Shock

Timing and Reasons Given

On December 2, 2016, merely five days after securing the World Championship at the Abu Dhabi Grand Prix, Nico Rosberg took to social media and a press conference in Vienna to announce his retirement from Formula 1. The timing of the announcement was as surprising as the decision itself. For many, it was inconceivable that a reigning World Champion, at the peak of his career and driving for the dominant Mercedes team, would choose to step away from the sport.

In his statement, Rosberg explained that achieving the World Championship had been a lifelong dream, one that required immense dedication, sacrifice, and effort. He spoke candidly about the intense pressures and challenges of competing at the highest level, particularly highlighting the mental and emotional toll of the 2016 season. The battle with Lewis Hamilton had pushed him to his limits, and reaching the pinnacle of success provided a sense of completion.

Rosberg cited a desire to prioritize his family life as a significant factor in his decision. Married to Vivian Sibold and father to their young daughter, he expressed a longing to spend more time with them. The relentless demands of Formula 1, with its grueling travel schedule and constant pursuit of performance, left little room for personal life. Rosberg emphasized that he wanted to be a present husband and father, roles that he deeply cherished.

He also acknowledged that continuing in the sport would require him to summon the same level of intensity and commitment, something he was no longer willing to do. "I have climbed my mountain, I am on the peak," Rosberg said. "So this feels right." By retiring at the top, he chose to close this chapter of his life on his own terms.

Reactions from the F1 Community

Surprise and Speculation

The announcement caught the entire Formula 1 community off guard. Team principals, fellow drivers, fans, and commentators expressed astonishment at Rosberg's decision. Toto Wolff, Mercedes' Team Principal, admitted that he was surprised but respected Rosberg's choice, describing it as "brave and testimony of the strength of his character."

Many within the paddock praised Rosberg for prioritizing his personal well-being and family. Jenson Button, who had announced his own step back from racing earlier that year, tweeted his support and understanding. Former champions like Alain Prost and Mika Häkkinen also commended Rosberg's decision, noting the immense pressures that come with the sport.

However, the suddenness of the retirement led to widespread speculation. Some wondered if the fierce rivalry with Hamilton had influenced Rosberg's choice. The intense psychological and emotional battles between the two, played out over several seasons, may have contributed to his desire to leave the sport. Others speculated about potential concerns over safety, given the inherent risks of racing.

Media outlets analyzed every aspect of the announcement, with some suggesting that Rosberg might have feared being unable to defend his title against Hamilton's relentless competitiveness. There were debates about whether retiring immediately after winning was an honorable exit or an evasion of future challenges.

Fans were divided in their reactions. While many respected Rosberg's decision to prioritize family and personal happiness, others expressed disappointment at not seeing a rematch between him and Hamilton in the following season. Social media platforms buzzed with discussions, tributes, and debates, reflecting the impact of Rosberg's departure on the global fanbase.

Hamilton's Response

Public Statements and Personal Feelings

Lewis Hamilton's response to Rosberg's retirement was a mix of surprise, respect, and underlying complexity reflective of their multifaceted relationship. In public statements, Hamilton congratulated Rosberg on his career and acknowledged the intensity of their rivalry. Speaking to the media at a sponsor event, he said, "This is the first time he's won in 18 years, hence why it was not a surprise that he decided to stop."

Hamilton also took to social media, posting a message that read: "Nico, congrats on your career. Good luck for whatever is ahead." The brevity of his message led some to speculate about his true feelings regarding Rosberg's departure.

Privately, Hamilton may have experienced a range of emotions. The rivalry with Rosberg had been a significant part of his career, pushing him to elevate his performance. Losing his primary competitor within the team could have been seen as both a relief and a disappointment. On one hand, it removed a formidable obstacle in his quest for future championships. On the other, the fierce competition had fueled his motivation, and Rosberg's exit meant the end of a defining chapter.

In interviews following the announcement, Hamilton hinted at mixed feelings. He expressed that he was looking forward to continuing the battle and that Rosberg's retirement "doesn't change anything" for his own approach. However, he also acknowledged the uniqueness of their shared history and the void that Rosberg's absence might create within the team dynamics.

Hamilton's comments reflected a professional demeanor, but underlying tensions from their past interactions seemed to linger. The nuances of their relationship—friendship turned rivalry, mutual respect tinged with personal conflicts—added layers to his response.

Legacy of the Decision

How It Affected Perceptions of Rosberg

Nico Rosberg's retirement immediately after winning the World Championship had a profound impact on how he was perceived within the sport. His decision was both lauded and critiqued, contributing to a complex legacy.

Admiration for Prioritizing Personal Values

Many admired Rosberg for choosing to retire at the pinnacle of his career. His willingness to step away from fame and potential future success to focus on family and personal fulfillment resonated with those who value balance and authenticity. It was seen as a courageous move, reflecting self-awareness and integrity.

Former drivers and industry insiders noted that few athletes have the opportunity or willingness to leave on such a high note. Rosberg's choice challenged the conventional narrative of relentless pursuit of more titles, highlighting that personal happiness can take precedence over professional accolades.

Criticism and Questions About Competitiveness

Conversely, some critics questioned whether Rosberg's retirement indicated an inability or unwillingness to defend his title against Hamilton. Detractors argued that stepping down immediately could be perceived as avoiding further competition, potentially diminishing the value of his championship.

Debates arose about the nature of true champions and whether Rosberg's decision aligned with the competitive spirit expected at the highest levels of sport. Comparisons were made to other champions who continued to fight for multiple titles, suggesting that his retirement left unanswered questions about his place among the greats.

Impact on His Legacy

Rosberg's legacy became a topic of rich discussion. His championship victory, achieved through perseverance and overcoming a formidable teammate, was a defining achievement. The retirement added a unique dimension, setting him apart in the history of Formula 1.

Some viewed his career as a complete arc, culminating perfectly with the title and a graceful exit. Others felt that his story was left unfinished, with potential unfulfilled. The duality of these perspectives ensured that Rosberg's name remained prominent in conversations about the sport's most intriguing figures.

Influence on Future Drivers

Rosberg's decision also had a ripple effect on how future drivers might approach their careers. It opened dialogues about mental health, personal priorities, and the pressures inherent in elite competition. His actions suggested that success could be defined individually and that stepping away does not equate to surrender but can be an expression of personal strength.

Mercedes' Adjustments

For the Mercedes team, Rosberg's retirement necessitated swift action to find a replacement. The unexpected vacancy led to the signing of Valtteri Bottas for the following season. Rosberg's departure altered the team dynamics and influenced strategic decisions moving forward.

Nico Rosberg's unexpected farewell from Formula 1 was a moment that transcended the usual narratives of the sport. It highlighted the human aspects behind the high-speed glamour—the personal choices, values, and sacrifices that define individuals beyond their professional achievements.

The timing and reasons for his retirement sparked widespread reactions, reflecting the complexity of his relationship with the sport, his teammate, and the fans. Lewis Hamilton's response added another layer to the story, encapsulating the nuanced interplay between rivalry and respect.

Rosberg's legacy, shaped by his championship win and immediate retirement, remains a subject of admiration, debate, and introspection within the Formula 1 community. His decision challenged traditional expectations and left an indelible mark on the sport's history.

In stepping away at the peak of his powers, Rosberg closed a significant chapter not only in his own life but also in the broader narrative of Formula 1. His farewell serves as a reminder that the paths athletes choose are deeply personal, influenced by a myriad of factors that extend beyond trophies and records. It underscores the profound impact that individual choices can have on perceptions, relationships, and the legacy one leaves behind.

Chapter 13: Aftermath and Individual Paths

The rivalry between Lewis Hamilton and Nico Rosberg not only defined an era in Formula 1 but also profoundly impacted their individual trajectories post-2016. With Rosberg stepping away from the sport and Hamilton continuing to chase records, their paths diverged significantly. This chapter explores Hamilton's continued dominance, Rosberg's new ventures, their reflections on the rivalry in later years, and how their story influenced future teammate dynamics in Formula 1.

Hamilton's Continued Success

Championships Won Post-2016

Following Nico Rosberg's unexpected retirement, Lewis Hamilton faced a new chapter in his career with Mercedes. The departure of his long-time rival altered the team dynamics, and Hamilton seized the opportunity to further solidify his legacy.

- **2017 Season**: Paired with new teammate Valtteri Bottas, Hamilton faced stiff competition from Ferrari's Sebastian Vettel. The season was a rollercoaster, with momentum shifting between Hamilton and Vettel. However, Hamilton's consistency and ability to capitalize on key moments led him to clinch his fourth World Championship with two races to spare.

- **2018 Season**: The battle with Vettel intensified. Despite early setbacks, Hamilton displayed exceptional form in the latter half of the season. He secured his fifth World Championship title, equaling Juan Manuel Fangio's record and further establishing himself among the sport's legends.

- **2019 Season**: Dominance continued as Hamilton won his sixth World Championship. The season saw him achieve multiple victories and podium finishes, showcasing not only his driving skill but also his strategic acumen during races.

- **2020 Season**: Amidst the global COVID-19 pandemic, the season was disrupted and shortened. Hamilton adapted seamlessly, winning his seventh World Championship and tying Michael Schumacher's all-time record. He broke numerous other records, including the most Grand Prix wins in history.

Evolving Legacy in F1

Lewis Hamilton's influence extended beyond his on-track achievements, shaping the culture and direction of Formula 1 in several significant ways.

- **Advocacy for Social Justice**: Hamilton became a leading voice for diversity and inclusion within the sport. He actively supported the Black Lives Matter movement, often taking a knee before races and wearing messages promoting equality. He established the **Hamilton Commission** to investigate the lack of diversity in motorsport and to recommend actions for change.

- **Environmental Initiatives**: Recognizing the environmental impact of racing, Hamilton adopted a plant-based lifestyle and promoted sustainability. He invested in eco-friendly projects and encouraged Formula 1 to move towards greener technologies.

- **Philanthropy and Entrepreneurship**: Hamilton engaged in various charitable endeavors, supporting education, health, and environmental causes. He ventured into business, launching a plant-based restaurant chain and collaborating on fashion lines that emphasized sustainability.

- **Recognition and Honors**: In 2021, Hamilton was knighted by Queen Elizabeth II for services to motorsport, becoming Sir Lewis Hamilton. His global popularity soared, transcending the sport and making him a cultural icon.

Hamilton's evolving legacy is characterized by his relentless pursuit of excellence, commitment to important social issues, and influence on future generations of drivers and fans.

Rosberg's New Ventures

Transition to Entrepreneurship and Punditry

Nico Rosberg's retirement marked the beginning of a new chapter focused on entrepreneurship, environmental advocacy, and media engagement.

- **Entrepreneurship and Investment**: Rosberg became an active investor in sustainable technologies and startups. He founded the **Greentech Festival**, an annual event promoting green innovation and sustainable living solutions. His investment portfolio included companies in electric mobility, renewable energy, and environmental sustainability.

- **Motorsport Involvement**: While no longer racing in Formula 1, Rosberg remained connected to motorsport through ventures like **Rosberg X Racing** in the Extreme E series. This off-road racing championship focuses on electric SUVs and aims to raise awareness about climate change and environmental challenges in remote locations.

- **Media and Punditry**: Rosberg transitioned into a media role, providing expert analysis and commentary for Formula 1 broadcasts. His insights, drawn from his experiences as a World Champion, added depth to race coverage. He appeared on networks like Sky Sports and maintained an active presence on YouTube, where he discussed racing strategies, technology, and industry developments.

- **Advocacy and Public Speaking**: Committed to environmental causes, Rosberg became a prominent advocate for sustainability. He engaged in public speaking events, sharing his perspectives on innovation, leadership, and the future of mobility.

Rosberg's post-racing career reflects a seamless integration of his passion for technology, sustainability, and communication. He redefined his professional identity while contributing positively to issues he cares deeply about.

Reflections on the Rivalry

Interviews and Comments in Later Years

In the years following their intense rivalry, both Hamilton and Rosberg have offered reflections that shed light on their experiences and personal growth.

Nico Rosberg:

- In various interviews, Rosberg acknowledged the immense mental and emotional effort required to compete against Hamilton. He described the 2016 season as all-consuming, stating that achieving the World Championship was the fulfillment of a lifelong ambition but came at a personal cost.

- Rosberg emphasized that retirement allowed him to focus on his family and pursue new passions without the relentless pressures of Formula 1. He expressed no regrets about his decision and often spoke about the importance of mental health and work-life balance.

- When discussing his relationship with Hamilton, Rosberg admitted that their friendship suffered during their rivalry but noted that time had helped heal some wounds. He expressed respect for Hamilton's continued success and occasionally praised his former teammate's achievements.

Lewis Hamilton:

- Hamilton has reflected on the rivalry as a defining period in his career. He acknowledged that competing against someone he had known since childhood added complexity to their professional relationship.

- In interviews, Hamilton has credited the rivalry with pushing him to elevate his performance. He recognized that the challenges posed by Rosberg forced him to develop resilience and adaptability.

- Regarding their personal relationship, Hamilton has indicated that while they may not be close friends, there is mutual respect. He has expressed understanding of Rosberg's decision to retire and appreciation for the intense competition they shared.

Shared Reflections:

- Both drivers have, at times, appeared together in media events or discussions, offering insights into their experiences. They have contributed to documentaries and retrospectives that analyze their rivalry, providing fans with a deeper understanding of the personal and professional dynamics involved.

- Their reflections often highlight themes of dedication, sacrifice, and the pursuit of excellence. They serve as candid accounts of what it takes to compete at the highest level of motorsport.

Impact on Future Teammate Dynamics

Lessons Learned by Teams and Drivers

The Hamilton-Rosberg rivalry had lasting implications for how Formula 1 teams and drivers approach internal competition.

Team Management Strategies:

- **Mercedes' Approach**: The team learned valuable lessons about managing two top-tier drivers. They implemented clearer communication channels, established firm guidelines on racing conduct, and emphasized team objectives over individual ambitions.

- **Balance of Competition and Collaboration**: Teams recognized the importance of fostering a healthy competitive environment while ensuring that rivalries did not compromise team harmony. Strategies included joint debriefings, team-building activities, and mediating conflicts promptly.

Driver Pairings Considerations:

- **Personality Compatibility**: Teams began to consider personality traits and interpersonal dynamics when selecting driver pairings. The aim was to minimize potential conflicts and promote constructive relationships.

- **Mentorship and Support**: Experienced drivers were encouraged to mentor younger teammates, shifting the dynamic from rivalry to collaboration. This approach helped in knowledge transfer and building team cohesion.

Emphasis on Mental Health:

- **Support Systems**: Recognizing the psychological pressures highlighted by the Hamilton-Rosberg rivalry, teams invested in mental health resources for drivers and staff. Access to sports psychologists and wellness programs became more common.

- **Open Dialogue**: Encouraging open communication about stress, burnout, and mental well-being helped create a supportive environment. Teams acknowledged that mental health was integral to performance.

Media and Public Relations Management:

- **Controlled Narratives**: Teams became more proactive in managing media interactions to prevent the amplification of internal tensions. They provided media training to drivers and established protocols for handling sensitive topics.
- **Unified Messaging**: Emphasizing team unity in public statements helped maintain a cohesive image and reduced speculation about internal conflicts.

Influence on Future Generations:

- **Role Models**: The Hamilton-Rosberg rivalry serves as a case study for aspiring drivers on handling competition and personal relationships within a team. It highlights the importance of professionalism, respect, and self-awareness.
- **Ethics and Sportsmanship**: The events during their rivalry prompted discussions about fair play, integrity, and the ethical considerations of competing against a teammate.

Technological and Strategic Adaptations:

- **Data Sharing Policies**: Teams reassessed policies on data sharing between drivers to ensure fairness while protecting sensitive information.
- **Strategic Decision-Making**: The need for clear and consistent strategies during races became evident, reducing ambiguities that could lead to conflicts.

The aftermath of the Hamilton-Rosberg rivalry illustrates how two individuals, starting from a shared dream, can forge vastly different paths shaped by personal choices, values, and experiences. Lewis Hamilton continued to redefine the boundaries of success in Formula 1, using his platform to advocate for broader societal issues and inspire future generations. Nico Rosberg embraced new challenges outside the cockpit, leveraging his knowledge and passion to make meaningful contributions to sustainability and innovation.

Their reflections on the rivalry offer valuable insights into the human aspects of high-level competition. They reveal the complexities of ambition, friendship, and personal fulfillment. The lessons learned have not only influenced their personal growth but have also left a lasting impact on how teams and drivers navigate the intricate dynamics of internal competition.

The legacy of their rivalry endures in the stories told, the records broken, and the changes inspired within the sport. It serves as a reminder that beyond the victories and accolades, it is the journey, the choices made, and the character displayed that truly define greatness.

Chapter 14: The Legacy of a Rivalry

The rivalry between Lewis Hamilton and Nico Rosberg transcended the confines of the racetrack, leaving an indelible mark on Formula 1 and the wider world of sports. Their intense competition from 2013 to 2016 not only shaped their careers but also influenced team management strategies, heightened the sport's global appeal, sparked cultural conversations, and inspired future generations of drivers. This chapter delves into the multifaceted legacy of their rivalry, examining its influence on Formula 1, a comparative analysis of their driving styles and achievements, and the cultural and social impacts that continue to resonate.

Influence on Formula 1

Changes in Team Management Approaches

The Hamilton-Rosberg rivalry presented Mercedes with unprecedented challenges in managing two top-tier drivers vying for the same championship within the same team. The intensity of their competition necessitated a reevaluation of traditional team management strategies in Formula 1, leading to innovations that have since influenced how teams operate.

Balancing Equality and Control

Mercedes initially adopted a policy of equal status for both drivers, providing them with identical equipment and opportunities. This approach was rooted in fairness but proved complex when their rivalry escalated. The team had to balance allowing the drivers to compete freely while maintaining overall team harmony and minimizing on-track incidents that could jeopardize results.

After the high-profile collisions in the 2014 Belgian Grand Prix and the 2016 Spanish Grand Prix, Mercedes introduced stricter guidelines. Team Principal Toto Wolff and Non-Executive Chairman Niki Lauda implemented measures such as:

- **Clear Codes of Conduct**: Establishing rules for on-track behavior between teammates, including how to race each other without compromising the team's interests.

- **Enhanced Communication**: Increasing dialogue between drivers and management to address grievances and prevent misunderstandings.

- **Strategic Team Orders**: In certain situations, the team prioritized strategic decisions over driver autonomy to secure maximum points.

These adjustments highlighted the necessity for teams to be agile in their management tactics, particularly when handling internal rivalries. Mercedes' experience became a case study for other teams facing similar dynamics, emphasizing the importance of proactive leadership and transparent policies.

Psychological Support and Human Factors

The rivalry also underscored the significance of psychological well-being in high-pressure environments. Mercedes recognized that mental resilience was as crucial as physical fitness, leading to:

- **Access to Sports Psychologists**: Providing professional support to help drivers cope with stress and maintain focus.

- **Team-Building Activities**: Fostering a sense of unity and mutual respect among all team members, including drivers, engineers, and support staff.

This holistic approach acknowledged that drivers are not just athletes but individuals whose mental state can profoundly impact performance. It set a precedent for incorporating psychological support into team structures.

Impact on Driver Pairings

The challenges faced by Mercedes influenced how other teams approached driver line-ups. Some teams began to consider not only the skill level of drivers but also their personalities and potential compatibility. The aim was to prevent destructive rivalries that could harm team cohesion and performance.

Impact on the Sport's Popularity

The Hamilton-Rosberg rivalry captivated audiences worldwide, elevating Formula 1's profile and contributing to its growth in popularity during their years of competition.

Compelling Storytelling

Their rivalry offered a narrative rich with drama: two childhood friends turned adversaries, competing at the pinnacle of motorsport. This storyline appealed to both dedicated fans and casual viewers, providing an emotional hook that transcended the technical aspects of racing.

Media outlets capitalized on this narrative, producing documentaries, in-depth analyses, and behind-the-scenes content. The heightened media attention expanded Formula 1's reach, attracting new fans and increasing engagement across platforms.

Global Audience Engagement

The rivalry coincided with Formula 1's efforts to expand into new markets, such as the United States and Asia. High-stakes duels between Hamilton and Rosberg added excitement to races, driving up television ratings and attendance figures. Social media buzzed with discussions, memes, and debates, fostering a vibrant online community.

Merchandising and Commercial Opportunities

Sponsorship deals and merchandising benefited from the rivalry. Brands associated with either driver or the team saw increased visibility. Merchandise sales, including team apparel and memorabilia, surged as fans rallied behind their preferred driver.

Influence on Race Regulations and Formats

The intense competition prompted discussions about race regulations, team orders, and the overall spectacle of Formula 1. The governing body, FIA, and stakeholders considered adjustments to enhance competitiveness and entertainment value, such as:

- **Regulation Changes**: Implementing rules to promote closer racing and reduce dominance by a single team.
- **Race Format Experiments**: Exploring ideas like reverse grids or sprint races to add unpredictability.

While not all proposed changes were adopted, the rivalry sparked conversations about the future direction of the sport.

Comparative Analysis

Driving Styles and Skill Sets

Despite driving identical machinery, Hamilton and Rosberg exhibited distinct driving styles and strengths that contributed to the intensity of their rivalry.

Lewis Hamilton

- **Natural Talent and Instinct**: Hamilton is often lauded for his raw speed and intuitive feel for the car. His ability to extract maximum performance, particularly in challenging conditions like rain, sets him apart.

- **Overtaking Prowess**: Known for bold and decisive overtaking maneuvers, Hamilton thrives in wheel-to-wheel combat, often making critical passes that change the course of a race.

- **Qualifying Excellence**: His exceptional qualifying record reflects his skill in delivering perfect laps under pressure, securing advantageous starting positions.

- **Mental Resilience**: Hamilton's confidence and psychological toughness enable him to rebound from setbacks and maintain focus during title battles.

Nico Rosberg

- **Technical Precision**: Rosberg's methodical approach emphasizes consistency and precision. His background in engineering contributes to a deep understanding of car setup and telemetry.

- **Strategic Thinking**: He excels in race strategy, tire management, and starts, often gaining positions off the line or through pit stop timing.

- **Work Ethic and Preparation**: Rosberg is known for his meticulous preparation, studying data extensively and refining every aspect of his performance.

- **Mental Preparation**: Investing in psychological training, Rosberg developed techniques to handle stress and maintain composure under pressure.

Head-to-Head Dynamics

Their differing styles led to contrasting strengths on various circuits and conditions. Hamilton often held the advantage in wet races and situations requiring aggressive overtaking, while Rosberg excelled on tracks where technical precision and strategy were paramount.

Their battles showcased the interplay of talent and approach:

- **2014 Bahrain Grand Prix**: A thrilling duel under the lights, with Hamilton defending against Rosberg's attacks, highlighting Hamilton's defensive skills and Rosberg's persistence.

- **2015 Spanish Grand Prix**: Rosberg's strategic mastery secured victory, demonstrating his ability to capitalize on qualifying and control the race pace.

Career Statistics and Records

Lewis Hamilton

- **World Championships**: Seven (2008, 2014, 2015, 2017, 2018, 2019, 2020)
- **Grand Prix Wins**: Over 100 victories, surpassing Michael Schumacher's record.
- **Pole Positions**: Holds the all-time record for pole positions.
- **Podium Finishes**: Over 170 podiums, reflecting remarkable consistency.

Nico Rosberg

- **World Championship**: One (2016)
- **Grand Prix Wins**: 23 victories during his career.
- **Pole Positions**: 30 pole positions, showcasing his qualifying speed.
- **Podium Finishes**: 57 podiums, illustrating sustained competitiveness.

Comparative Achievements

While Hamilton's statistics place him among the greatest drivers in history, Rosberg's accomplishments are significant, particularly considering his decision to retire at the peak of his career.

Their head-to-head record during their time as teammates (2013-2016) was closely contested:

- **Wins**: Hamilton had 32 victories; Rosberg had 22.

- **Pole Positions**: Hamilton secured 35 poles; Rosberg had 29.

- **Fastest Laps**: Both drivers frequently set fastest laps, with Hamilton slightly ahead.

These figures underscore the fierce competition between them, with each pushing the other to new heights.

Cultural and Social Impact

Representation and Diversity Discussions

Lewis Hamilton's Influence

As the first and only Black driver in Formula 1, Hamilton's success brought issues of diversity and inclusion to the forefront of the sport.

- **Breaking Barriers**: Hamilton's rise challenged the perception of Formula 1 as an exclusive domain, inspiring individuals from diverse backgrounds to pursue careers in motorsport.

- **Advocacy**: He became an outspoken advocate for racial equality and social justice, using his platform to highlight systemic issues and support movements like Black Lives Matter.

- **The Hamilton Commission**: In 2020, Hamilton launched an initiative to identify and address the barriers preventing Black people from participating in UK motorsport, aiming to create sustainable change.

Impact on Formula 1

Hamilton's activism prompted Formula 1 to reflect on its own practices:

- **#WeRaceAsOne Campaign**: The sport introduced initiatives to promote diversity, inclusion, and sustainability.

- **Diversity and Inclusion Efforts**: Teams began implementing programs to encourage participation from underrepresented groups, including scholarships and internships.

Nico Rosberg's Contribution

While not as prominently associated with diversity discussions, Rosberg's multicultural background (German-Finnish heritage, raised in Monaco) and multilingual abilities highlighted the international nature of the sport.

Role Model Status for Aspiring Drivers

Lewis Hamilton

Hamilton's journey from humble beginnings to becoming one of the most successful drivers in history serves as a powerful inspiration:

- **Perseverance and Determination**: His story demonstrates the importance of dedication, hard work, and resilience in overcoming obstacles.

- **Authenticity**: Hamilton's openness about his personal experiences, interests in fashion and music, and commitment to causes outside racing make him relatable to a broader audience.

- **Mentorship**: He actively supports young drivers, offering guidance and encouragement.

Nico Rosberg

Rosberg's approach to his career offers valuable lessons:

- **Work-Life Balance**: His decision to retire at the peak of his career emphasizes the importance of personal fulfillment and family.

- **Entrepreneurship and Innovation**: Post-retirement, Rosberg pursued ventures in sustainability and technology, showing how athletes can leverage their platform for broader impact.

- **Mental Wellness**: His candid discussions about the psychological pressures of racing contribute to destigmatizing mental health conversations.

Inspiring Future Generations

Both drivers have left a lasting legacy that motivates aspiring racers:

- **Diversity and Inclusion**: Hamilton's presence encourages young people from underrepresented communities to pursue their passion for motorsport.

- **Holistic Development**: Rosberg's emphasis on education, technical knowledge, and personal well-being highlights the importance of a well-rounded approach.

The legacy of the Hamilton-Rosberg rivalry is profound and multifaceted. It reshaped team management strategies, influenced the sport's popularity, and sparked important cultural and social conversations. Their intense competition not only pushed each other to achieve greater heights but also captivated audiences worldwide, elevating Formula 1's global appeal.

Their contrasting driving styles and skill sets provided thrilling spectacles on the track and enriched the sport's competitive landscape. The statistical records and achievements of both drivers reflect their exceptional talents and the high stakes of their rivalry.

Culturally, the rivalry contributed to vital discussions about representation, diversity, and the role of athletes as agents of change. Hamilton's advocacy for social justice and Rosberg's focus on sustainability and mental wellness demonstrate how sports figures can leverage their influence beyond their primary domain.

As role models, they have inspired countless individuals to pursue their dreams, emphasizing that success is multifaceted and personal fulfillment is as important as professional accolades.

In the annals of Formula 1 history, the Hamilton-Rosberg rivalry stands as a testament to the complexities of human competition, the possibilities unleashed when talent meets opportunity, and the enduring impact that two individuals can have on a global stage. Their legacy continues to shape the sport, influence future generations, and remind us of the extraordinary narratives that unfold when passion and ambition converge.

Chapter 15: Lessons in Competition and Friendship

The story of Lewis Hamilton and Nico Rosberg is not just a chronicle of two talented drivers battling for supremacy in Formula 1; it is also a profound exploration of the complexities of human relationships under the strain of intense competition. Their journey from childhood friends to fierce rivals and beyond offers valuable insights into the thin line that separates teammates from adversaries, the role of sportsmanship and ethics in high-stakes environments, and the personal growth that emerges from facing such challenges. This chapter delves into the lessons learned from their rivalry, shedding light on how competition affects relationships, the ethical debates their actions sparked, and how their experiences shaped their characters.

The Thin Line Between Teammates and Rivals

How Competition Affects Relationships

Lewis Hamilton and Nico Rosberg's relationship began in the karting circuits of Europe when they were young boys with big dreams. Their friendship was built on mutual respect, shared ambitions, and the joy of racing. As teammates in karting and later in Formula 1 with Mercedes, they found themselves in a unique position: collaborators working towards a common goal while simultaneously competing for individual glory.

The transition from friends to rivals was gradual but inevitable as they both ascended to the pinnacle of motorsport. The intense pressure to perform, coupled with the desire to outshine each other, began to strain their relationship. The dynamics of their friendship changed as they navigated the challenges of competing for the same accolades.

Competition can amplify underlying tensions in any relationship, and in the case of Hamilton and Rosberg, it highlighted the delicate balance between personal ambition and mutual respect. The proximity of their rivalry—sharing the same team, engineers, and equipment—meant that every advantage gained by one was perceived as a loss by the other. This environment bred an atmosphere where trust was difficult to maintain.

Key moments that tested their relationship included on-track incidents such as the collision at the 2014 Belgian Grand Prix and the controversial qualifying session at Monaco the same year. These events not only impacted their standings in the championship but also eroded the foundation of their friendship. Misunderstandings and perceived slights became more pronounced, leading to a breakdown in communication.

Their experience illustrates how competition can alter the dynamics of even the closest relationships. The pursuit of success often requires a level of self-focus that can conflict with the collaborative aspects of being part of a team. In high-pressure environments, the line between teammate and rival becomes blurred, and navigating this boundary requires emotional intelligence, open communication, and a commitment to shared values.

Hamilton and Rosberg's journey shows that while competition can drive individuals to excel, it can also create rifts if not managed carefully. Their story serves as a cautionary tale about the potential cost of unchecked rivalry and the importance of maintaining perspective on what truly matters in relationships.

Sportsmanship and Ethics

Debates Sparked by Their Actions

The rivalry between Hamilton and Rosberg was not only a battle of speed and strategy but also a contest of sportsmanship and ethical conduct. Their actions on and off the track ignited debates within the Formula 1 community and among fans worldwide, raising questions about the lengths to which competitors should go in pursuit of victory.

One of the most significant incidents that sparked ethical debates was the 2014 Monaco Grand Prix qualifying session. Rosberg's off-track excursion resulted in yellow flags that prevented Hamilton from completing his flying lap. While the stewards cleared Rosberg of any wrongdoing, suspicions lingered about whether the move was intentional. The incident highlighted the fine line between tactical acumen and unsportsmanlike behavior.

Similarly, the collision at the 2016 Spanish Grand Prix, where both drivers were eliminated on the first lap after a clash, prompted discussions about responsibility and aggression. Was it a racing incident born out of competitive zeal, or did it reflect a deeper disregard for mutual respect?

Hamilton's tactics during the 2016 Abu Dhabi Grand Prix also drew scrutiny. Deliberately slowing the pace to back Rosberg into other competitors, Hamilton defied team instructions in a last-ditch effort to win the championship. Some praised his strategic ingenuity, while others criticized his disregard for team directives and the potential risks involved.

These events led to broader conversations about the ethical boundaries in sports. Is winning at all costs acceptable, or should there be limits to competitive behavior? The debates extended to topics such as:

- **Team Orders vs. Individual Ambition**: The balance between following team strategies and pursuing personal goals became a contentious issue. Should drivers prioritize the team's interests over their own, especially when a championship is at stake?

- **Fair Play and Integrity**: Actions perceived as underhanded or manipulative raised questions about the integrity of the sport. Fans and commentators debated whether certain tactics undermined the spirit of fair competition.

- **Responsibility to the Sport**: As high-profile athletes, Hamilton and Rosberg had a responsibility to uphold the values of Formula 1. Their conduct influenced public perception and set examples for aspiring drivers.

The ethical dilemmas presented by their rivalry underscored the complexity of professional sports, where the desire to win can conflict with principles of sportsmanship. Their actions served as catalysts for discussions about what constitutes acceptable behavior and the moral obligations of competitors.

Ultimately, the debates sparked by Hamilton and Rosberg's rivalry contributed to a deeper understanding of sports ethics. They highlighted the need for clear guidelines, open dialogue, and a shared commitment to upholding the integrity of the competition.

Personal Growth and Maturity

How the Rivalry Shaped Their Characters

The intense rivalry between Hamilton and Rosberg was a crucible that forged significant personal growth and maturity in both men. The challenges they faced, both in competition and in managing their relationship, compelled them to reflect, adapt, and evolve.

Lewis Hamilton emerged from the rivalry with a renewed sense of purpose and a broader perspective on his role both within and beyond the sport. The struggles and conflicts with Rosberg prompted him to:

- **Develop Emotional Resilience**: Dealing with setbacks, criticism, and the breakdown of a close friendship required Hamilton to build emotional strength. He learned to channel negative experiences into motivation, refining his mental approach to competition.

- **Enhance Leadership Skills**: Navigating team dynamics and public scrutiny pushed Hamilton to become a more effective communicator and leader within Mercedes. He recognized the importance of collaboration and worked to foster positive relationships with his team.

- **Expand His Influence**: The rivalry motivated Hamilton to look beyond personal accolades, leading him to engage in social and environmental causes. His advocacy for diversity, equality, and sustainability reflects a maturation that extends his impact beyond racing.

Nico Rosberg, through the trials of competing against Hamilton, experienced profound personal transformation. The rivalry led him to:

- **Prioritize Personal Values**: Recognizing the toll that the competition was taking on his personal life, Rosberg chose to retire at the peak of his career. This decision demonstrated a commitment to his family and personal well-being over professional pursuits.

- **Cultivate Self-Awareness**: Facing the pressures of rivalry required Rosberg to deeply understand his strengths and limitations. He invested in psychological training and self-improvement, which not only enhanced his performance but also his personal development.

- **Embrace New Opportunities**: Post-retirement, Rosberg channeled his competitive drive into entrepreneurship and advocacy. His ventures in sustainability and technology reflect a shift towards purpose-driven endeavors that align with his values.

Their rivalry forced both men to confront aspects of themselves that might have remained unexamined in less demanding circumstances. The challenges they faced catalyzed growth in areas such as emotional intelligence, ethical judgment, and personal priorities.

Moreover, the experiences shaped their perspectives on competition and success. They learned that winning is multifaceted and that personal fulfillment often requires balancing ambition with other aspects of life. The rivalry taught them about sacrifice, integrity, and the importance of staying true to oneself.

In later years, both Hamilton and Rosberg have reflected on how their rivalry contributed to their personal journeys. While it strained their friendship, it also provided invaluable lessons that have influenced their paths and the ways they engage with the world.

Their stories exemplify how intense competition can be a powerful catalyst for personal growth. By facing and overcoming challenges, individuals can develop resilience, wisdom, and a deeper understanding of themselves and others.

The legacy of Lewis Hamilton and Nico Rosberg's rivalry extends far beyond their achievements on the track. It offers profound insights into the complexities of human relationships, the ethical dimensions of competition, and the potential for personal transformation under pressure.

Their journey illustrates that the line between teammates and rivals is delicate and requires careful navigation to preserve relationships amidst competition. The debates sparked by their actions highlight the ongoing importance of sportsmanship and ethics in professional sports. Perhaps most importantly, their experiences demonstrate how rivalry can lead to significant personal growth, shaping individuals in ways that transcend their professional accomplishments.

As their stories continue to inspire and provoke thought, the lessons learned from their rivalry remain relevant. They serve as a reminder that competition and friendship, while often in tension, can coexist when approached with integrity, respect, and a commitment to personal and mutual growth.

Conclusion: The Enduring Tale of Hamilton vs. Rosberg

The saga of Lewis Hamilton and Nico Rosberg is a compelling narrative that encapsulates the essence of competition, friendship, and personal growth within the high-octane world of Formula 1. Their journey, marked by intense rivalries, mutual respect, and profound personal decisions, offers a multifaceted story that resonates beyond the racetrack. As we reflect on their intertwined careers, several key takeaways emerge, illuminating universal themes that transcend the sport and speak to the very core of the human spirit.

Summarizing Their Story

Key Takeaways from Their Journey

Lewis Hamilton and Nico Rosberg's relationship began in the karting circuits of Europe, where young talents met and forged a friendship based on a shared passion for racing. Their paths, however, took divergent turns as they ascended the ranks of motorsport. Hamilton's meteoric rise with McLaren and subsequent dominance with Mercedes contrasted with Rosberg's steady progression, culminating in his solitary World Championship in 2016.

Their reunion at Mercedes in 2013 reignited their rivalry, transforming their friendship into a fierce competition for supremacy within the same team. The seasons that followed were characterized by remarkable performances, strategic battles, and moments of both triumph and contention. Incidents like the collisions in Monaco and Belgium, the cap-throwing at the U.S. Grand Prix, and the dramatic finale in Abu Dhabi underscored the intensity of their competition.

Rosberg's unexpected retirement shortly after his championship victory added a poignant chapter to their story, highlighting the personal costs of relentless ambition. Meanwhile, Hamilton continued to break records and champion social causes, evolving into a global icon whose influence extends far beyond racing.

The Nature of Rivalries in Sport

Universal Themes and Insights

The Hamilton-Rosberg rivalry serves as a microcosm of the broader dynamics that define competition in sports. Several universal themes emerge from their story, offering insights into the nature of rivalries and their impact on individuals and organizations.

1. The Thin Line Between Teammates and Rivals: Their journey illustrates how competition can both strengthen and strain relationships. As teammates, Hamilton and Rosberg had to navigate the delicate balance of cooperation and competition, where mutual success depended on both individuals' performances. Their rivalry exemplifies how close competition can foster excellence while also creating tensions that challenge personal bonds.

2. Sportsmanship and Ethics: Their actions on and off the track sparked debates about sportsmanship and ethical conduct in high-stakes environments. Incidents that tested their integrity and respect for each other highlighted the ethical dilemmas athletes face when ambition clashes with fairness. Their story underscores the importance of maintaining ethical standards to preserve the spirit of competition.

3. Personal Sacrifices and Growth: The rivalry demanded significant personal sacrifices from both drivers, shaping their characters and life choices. Their experiences reveal how intense competition can drive individuals to achieve greatness while also necessitating profound personal growth and introspection.

4. Media Influence and Public Perception: The role of the media in amplifying their rivalry demonstrates how external narratives can influence and sometimes exacerbate internal dynamics. The media's portrayal of their competition affected public perception, adding pressure and shaping the legacy of their rivalry.

Final Thoughts

What Their Rivalry Tells Us About Ambition, Success, and the Human Spirit

The Hamilton-Rosberg rivalry is more than a tale of two drivers vying for championships; it is a profound exploration of ambition, success, and the complexities of the human spirit.

1. Ambition as a Double-Edged Sword: Ambition propelled both drivers to extraordinary heights, driving them to excel and innovate. However, it also created friction and personal challenges, illustrating that ambition, while a powerful motivator, can have both positive and negative consequences. Their story highlights the need for balance—pursuing goals with passion while maintaining personal well-being and relationships.

2. Redefining Success: Success in their narrative is multifaceted. For Hamilton, it encompasses not only race victories and championships but also his advocacy for social justice and environmental sustainability. For Rosberg, success culminates in achieving his championship dream and making the difficult choice to retire in pursuit of personal fulfillment. Their differing definitions of success emphasize that true achievement is deeply personal and extends beyond professional accolades.

3. Resilience and Adaptability: Both drivers demonstrated remarkable resilience in the face of setbacks and adaptability in evolving their careers post-rivalry. Hamilton's continued success and Rosberg's transition to entrepreneurship and advocacy reflect their ability to navigate change and redefine their identities beyond racing.

4. The Human Spirit: Their rivalry underscores the resilience of the human spirit—the capacity to strive for excellence, overcome adversity, and grow through challenges. It speaks to the universal experience of pursuing one's passions while grappling with the complexities that come with intense competition.

5. Legacy and Inspiration: The enduring legacy of Hamilton and Rosberg's rivalry lies in its ability to inspire future generations. Their story serves as a powerful reminder that greatness is not solely measured by titles but also by the courage to make difficult choices, the willingness to push boundaries, and the commitment to personal values.

Conclusion

The tale of Lewis Hamilton and Nico Rosberg is an enduring narrative that captures the essence of what it means to compete at the highest level while navigating the intricate dynamics of personal relationships and ethical considerations. Their journey offers invaluable lessons on the nature of rivalry, the pursuit of success, and the importance of maintaining one's integrity and humanity amidst fierce competition.

As Formula 1 continues to evolve, the legacy of Hamilton and Rosberg's rivalry remains a benchmark for excellence and a testament to the profound impact that competition can have on individuals and the sport as a whole. Their story is a celebration of the human spirit's capacity to strive for greatness, adapt to change, and inspire others to pursue their dreams with unwavering passion and integrity.

In the annals of motorsport history, the Hamilton-Rosberg rivalry stands out not only for its competitive intensity but also for the deeper reflections it provokes about ambition, success, and the intricate dance between friendship and rivalry. It is a story that will be remembered and studied for years to come, embodying the timeless truths about what it takes to be truly great in the face of relentless competition.

About the Author

Etienne Psaila, an accomplished author with over two decades of experience, has mastered the art of weaving words across various genres. His journey in the literary world has been marked by a diverse array of publications, demonstrating not only his versatility but also his deep understanding of different thematic landscapes. However, it's in the realm of automotive literature that Etienne truly combines his passions, seamlessly blending his enthusiasm for cars with his innate storytelling abilities.

Specializing in automotive and motorcycle books, Etienne brings to life the world of automobiles through his eloquent prose and an array of stunning, high-quality color photographs. His works are a tribute to the industry, capturing its evolution, technological advancements, and the sheer beauty of vehicles in a manner that is both informative and visually captivating.

A proud alumnus of the University of Malta, Etienne's academic background lays a solid foundation for his meticulous research and factual accuracy. His education has not only enriched his writing but has also fueled his career as a dedicated teacher. In the classroom, just as in his writing, Etienne strives to inspire, inform, and ignite a passion for learning.

As a teacher, Etienne harnesses his experience in writing to engage and educate, bringing the same level of dedication and excellence to his students as he does to his readers. His dual role as an educator and author makes him uniquely positioned to understand and convey complex concepts with clarity and ease, whether in the classroom or through the pages of his books.

Through his literary works, Etienne Psaila continues to leave an indelible mark on the world of automotive literature, captivating car enthusiasts and readers alike with his insightful perspectives and compelling narratives.

Visit www.etiennepsaila.com for more.